# Transforming Your Students into Deep Learners

## A Guide for Instructors

Charlie Sweet, Hal Blythe, Bill Phillips, & Russell Carpenter

NEW FORUMS PRESS INC.
Published in the United States of America
by New Forums Press, Inc.1018 S. Lewis St.
Stillwater, OK 74074
www.newforums.com

Copyright © 2016 by New Forums Press, Inc.

All rights reserved. No part of this publication may be reproduced or transmitted in any form or by any means, electronic or mechanical, including photocopy, or any information storage or retrieval system, without permission in writing from the publisher.

Library of Congress Cataloging-in-Publication Data Pending

This book may be ordered in bulk quantities at discount from New Forums Press, Inc., P.O. Box 876, Stillwater, OK 74076 [Federal I.D. No. 73 1123239]. Printed in the United States of America.

ISBN 10: 1-58107-294-5
ISBN 13: 978-1-58107-294-5

# Table of Contents

**PREFACE** ..................................................................................................... v

**BACKGROUND TO DEEP LEARNING** ............................................... 1
1. Introduction ................................................................................................ 3
2. Deep Learning vs. Surface Learning ........................................................ 7
3. The Making of Academic Surfers: Characteristics of Today's
    Entering College Students and Culture That Hinder
    Deep Learning ....................................................................................... 15
4. The Learning Gap ................................................................................... 25

**EIGHT EXCELLENT STRATEGIES FOR DEEP LEARNING:
    Using BRIDLE** .................................................................................... 27
5. STRATEGY I: Climbing Bloom's Staircase ........................................... 29
6. STRATEGY II: Presenting for Deep Learning ....................................... 37
7. STRATEGY III: Facilitating Retrieving for Deep Learning ................. 45
8. STRATEGY IV: Fostering Metacognition for Deep Learning ............. 53
9. STRATEGY V: Developing Critical Thinking for Deep Learning ...... 65
10. STRATEGY VI: Employing Deep Reading for Deep Learning .......... 75
11. STRATEGY VII: Creating Spaces for Deep Learning ......................... 81
12. STRATEGY VIII: Motivating Students to be Deep Learners ............. 87

**HONING YOUR SKILLS** ..................................................................... 95
13. Conclusion ............................................................................................. 97
14. Appendix A: **BRIDLE**: A Systematic Plan for
    Self-Improvement in Promoting Deep Learning .............................. 99
15. Appendix B: A Selected, Partially Annotated Bibliography .............. 105
16. Appendix C: ARTS, A Student Learning Skills Inventory ................ 111

About the Authors ..................................................................................... 113

# PREFACE

When we wrote *Achieving Excellence in Teaching* (*AET*) back in 2014, we had no thought of a sequel, no *Son of Achieving Excellence in Teaching*, but we forgot to take into account Newton's Third Law of Motion. Every time Bill taught his College Teaching course (EDL 830), whether live or in an online format, he received the same reaction: students would ask him for a broader explanation of Chapter 3, "Deep Learning." Likewise, when we facilitated conference presentations based on *AET*, the first question we received invariably dealt with students' achieving deep learning. Maybe the reactions to our book weren't exactly the Newtonian "equal" and "opposite," but our colleagues and students did make us aware of a definite desire for an expanded discussion of this primal pedagogical principle.

We had pointed out in Chapter 3 of *AET* that college students have a tendency to choose surface learning over deep learning, but instructors "want to encourage them to choose the latter" (11). We realized that we needed to do a better job of explaining why students make such a choice and how excellent teachers could not only "encourage" but foster deep learning.

Moreover, through teaching, committee work, and discussion, we became very much aware that high school students were not prepared to perform college-level work. **Maybe it wasn't so much that college students chose surface learning as that they were conditioned to approach learning in this fashion.**

Professional developers believe passionately that following best practices will allow faculty to lead their students toward deep learning, and we felt we needed to spell out those practices, right down to the most effective exercises. While constructing longitudinal studies that demonstrate that our teaching Professor S Strategy Y will lead to deep learning in Student A is a Holy Grail we will never attain, we have reviewed the most recent research on deep learning, especially from the brain scientists, and experimented with the concepts we discovered.

Since teaching and learning remain two sides of the same coin, think of *AET* and this book as companion pieces. If you haven't yet read *AET*, by all means finish this book, and then go back and read *AET*. The momentum will propel you toward excellence.

And don't forget what Newton's first law told us about a body in motion.

# Part I

## Background to Deep Learning

# I. Introduction

Years ago when Bill was beginning at Cypress Springs Elementary School in Ruston, Louisiana, he taught his students the traditional three Rs--reading, writing, and `rithmetic. He established a fourth R, rapport, with his students, planned his lessons expertly, fostered a high level of enthusiasm, and, as a result, the kids seemed to be learning. By Christmas break Bill proudly thought he must be in the upper ten percent of all teachers. Then the school district "invited" him to give a comprehensive exam before the Christmas break and give the exam again after the Christmas break to see if students retained the knowledge they had acquired. His students had impressive results on the pre-test, but unexpectedly dismal results on the post-test.

How could this sharp fall-off in retention be possible? How could he be a brilliant new teacher who helped students move forward with their learning and then, in just three short weeks, become such a failure? What had he done wrong, and how could he help students learn in such a way that they could not only remember material over time but actually learn it?

After much reflection and substantial research, Bill concluded that his teaching techniques created something Nicholas Carr refers to as shallow learning. In *The Shallows* (2010), Carr postulates that the Internet, like Bill's teaching, is causing people, who spend an average of twelve seconds on a website, to wade through a plethora of shallow information, circumventing the ability to read effectively and think deeply. As Carr labels these Internet users "pancake people," let's refer to their educational counterparts as **pancake students**.

Even before the advent of the Internet, Bill came to the epiphany that he was teaching in the shallows at Cypress Springs Elementary--he was not helping students make connections, students were not filing information in their brains in a manner that allowed for easy retrieval, and short-term memories were not being stored in long-term memory—i.e., no deep learning. His new perspective caused him to realize he was mired in the bottom of Bloom's Taxonomy, teaching factual information without having his students use the information in a meaningful way. His kids were not evaluating the information, not creating anything new with the knowledge, not making connections with other fields of knowledge. They were learning for the test and then forgetting. New knowledge was constantly being introduced, and old information was being dropped rather than being used as a solid foundation on which to build.

Bill realized the learning process he was inculcating in his students might be compared to putting marbles on a plate. The plate, like short-term memory, has just so much space. It is wide but shallow and in this example can hold only forty-nine marbles. When the fiftieth marble goes on the plate, one of the other marbles has to fall off the plate. Teaching an inch deep and a mile wide, Bill lacked the skill and experience to conduct a class in a manner where deep learning occurred. His students achieved immediate, but not long-term learning.

Unfortunately, Bill was not alone. Many teachers lack the awareness, knowledge, training, and skills to help students learn in a way that ensures the knowledge endures. Professors often fill their students with information, but don't ask them to use the knowledge in a meaningful, active way in real-life scenarios.

Today's college students arrive on campus conditioned by a testing mania that contributes to this desire to instill knowledge students can spit back whether the test is called an ACT, a remnant of No Child Left Behind, or even Common Core. Teaching to the test becomes the default pedagogy. Because grading multiple-choice tests is easy, especially compared to creating essay rubrics and training others to use them, high school classes many times are organized around easily score-able material—convergent answers.

Simply put, K-12 teaching emphasizes shallow/surface learning—colleges and universities, on the other hand, should demand deep learning. Said another way, **high school students are not prepared to learn in higher education classes.**

The purpose of this book is to provide you with a working knowledge of deep learning, to differentiate this level from surface learning, to explain why teaching toward deep learning is important, and to offer the best ways for implementing this teaching so as to transform your students from short- to long-term learners. A rubric for deep learning strategies we call BRIDLE will be provided for you to evaluate your teaching skills in order to determine whether or not they promote such deep learning. You are invited to use the BRIDLE to identify and create a set of skills that, when used properly, will help your students learn materials that will be embedded in their brains for a long time.

Sound hard? Remember how difficult it was when you first learned to ride a bike? Your age was in single digits and your brain not fully formed, yet you learned a myriad of inter-related skills. Bicyclists have to master the balance, the steering, the locomotion, all at the same time in varied situations: across the grass, on the sidewalk, in the street, and off the curb. Bicyclists ride several types of bikes, in groups or by themselves, and often fall off, bump into someone else, or crash. They are engaged in active learning, with intrinsic value and used in diverse settings—in short, deep learning. Regardless of how long it's been since

*Many teachers lack the awareness, knowledge, training, and skills to help students learn in a way that ensures the knowledge endures.*

you've ridden one, you can get on any bike, in any situation, and do it again without further instruction.

Shouldn't what happens in academia work at least as effectively as learning to ride a bike?

# 2. Deep Learning vs. Surface Learning

**LEARNING QUIZ** (True or False)

1. Deep learners are always deep learners, and surface learners are always surface learners.

2. Research into deep learning is a 21$^{st}$-century development.

3. Motivation is unimportant in whether students choose to be surface or deep learners.

4. Deep learners tend to connect new knowledge with old.

5. Deep learners employ only higher order cognitive skills.

## BACKGROUND

In our *Achieving Excellence in Teaching* (2014), Chapter 3 focused on deep learning primarily as a strategy for highly effective teachers, who, we claimed, "foster deep learning. Students who are asked on a daily basis to apply analyze, evaluate, create, and reflect are more apt to be transformed into deep learners" (15). That book was aimed at an audience of instructors. Obviously, we enumerated some pedagogical strategies that we did not have time to explore in depth. We hinted at why some students choose surface learning, but we did not explore the contexts and research. One reason for writing *Transforming Your Students Into Deep Learners*, as we suggested earlier, is to hatch some embryos left nesting in our previous book.

Also, at our institution we have begun to implement some strategies from our 2014 book, and our experience has become much more than theoretical. Last year, for instance, we worked on an assessment committee that rewrote our unit's strategic plan so as to position deep learning as our major objective (see http://noelstudio/assessment). At all our August orientations (i.e., New Faculty, Part-time Faculty, Teaching Assistants, First-Year Course Instructors), we stressed that while "Excellence in Teaching Is Job One," its end purpose is deep learning on the part of our students.

Before launching into a discussion of those strategies that promote deep learning, however, we need to provide some background on the aforementioned learning approaches—surface and deep—detailing their similarities and differences, their strengths and weaknesses, what they seek to achieve and how they attempt to achieve it.

## SURFACE LEARNING

Surface and deep learning lie at opposite ends of the study spectrum, but that doesn't necessarily mean a student can be always classified as a surface or deep learner. Charlie, for instance, was a surface learner when it came to the sciences and accounting (a course his father insisted he take in college), but a deep learner when it came to the literature of any nation at any time. Charlie simply did not care about the former fields, but grew passionate about the latter. The major point here is that motivation has much to do with learning approaches.

Research on deep/surface learning has focused on both the teacher and the student, sometimes even exploring their intertwined roles in the learning process. We appreciate the teacher-student nomenclature as both can be learners. Deep and surface learning began to show up in educational research journals in the 1970s, due mainly to the work being done by Marton and Saljo in Sweden and Ramsden and Entwistle in Australia and the UK. As Rhem (2009-10) indicates, "the deep/surface researchers concentrated on observing commonalities. How did actual students actually study and what were the environmental cues that prompted them to take the approach ('deep' or 'surface') they chose? ... The research found that students' intention in studying/learning relates strongly to their perceptions of *what* they will be assessed on and *how* they will be assessed." Note the early research centered more on how a student learns than how an instructor teaches, and, as Rocconi et al (2014) convey, deep learners retain information longer, earn higher grades, seem more satisfied with the learning process, develop critical thinking skills, and integrate and transfer information at higher rates.

Focusing on the instructor, Entwistle (1988) indicates that teachers who create surface learning often rush to cover too much material, emphasizing coverage at the expense of depth and assigning busy work with low expectations. These teachers think that everything in the book has equal value and cover the material like a slow moving river that is a mile wide and an inch deep. It is important for each teacher to determine what matters most and to take the time to create assignments that make students apply what has been learned.

Concerned with the student, Bowden and Marton (1998) postulate that a surface approach to learning is motivated by avoiding failure while failing to make connections, relationships, and application. Both the teacher and the learner are focused on test taking. Test taking is an important aspect of education, and it is the design of the test questions and the application of new knowledge that make the difference. A good test question will ask the

> *Surface and deep learning lie at opposite ends of the study spectrum, but that doesn't necessarily mean a student can be always classified as a surface or deep learner.*

learner to apply the new knowledge, to compare and contrast, to analyze, or create a product based on the new information. Simply memorizing and repeating and forgetting causes surface learning.

McDrury and Alterio (2002), likewise centered on the student, believe that surface learning is a restrictive strategy focused on completing a particular assignment, which is soon forgotten and not connected. Some college students jump from assignment to assignment, from course to course, and from semester to semester without connecting the new knowledge. The purpose of a liberal education is to create critical and creative thinkers who can apply knowledge across disciplines, but that application too rarely occurs. The typical college student is focused on one assignment at a time, and few take the initiative to connect the dots through reflection and metacognition.

Interested in how students prepare for assessment, Biggs and Tang (2007) define surface learning as cramming to pass the test by relying on rote memory. This insight is particularly relative to today's world of high stakes testing, where teachers and administrators are held accountable for raising test scores. Therefore, teachers plan lessons and exams that focus on memorization of facts or a formula that will be on the test. This action then fills the minimum requirements for teachers and administrators to keep their jobs and for students to pass the test.

According to Millis (2010), who examines the teacher-student dichotomy, surface learning is memorizing unquestioned material that is not connected. Excellent teachers help students make connections and explore why the information is important. Connecting one class to another and one field to another is critical to developing understanding. Students yearn to know why information is important and how to make sense of their world. They want to explore the connections, yet novice teachers too often move on after basic facts have been mastered.

Millis (2014) also suggests that surface learners study superficially to memorize facts, which remain unquestioned and unconnected. They do not examine key underlying principles, do not connect old knowledge to new, do not engage, rely on old thinking, lack the ability to generalize, concern themselves with how they will be tested, and generally dislike learning.

## DEEP LEARNING

Over the past forty years researchers have studied deep learning, realizing that its tenets and effects are at times shockingly different from those of surface learning. Marton and Saljo (1976) discovered that student deep learners read for overall understanding and meaning. Perhaps the most succinct—but nonetheless thorough—definition of deep learning comes from Drummer et al (2008): "Deep learning refers to learning that encom-

> *The purpose of a liberal education is to create critical and creative thinkers who can apply knowledge across disciplines, but that application too rarely occurs.*

passes the acquisition and application of higher order skills, such as analyzing, interpreting and evaluating information (Hill & Woodland, 2002), with the aim of encouraging students to modify or evaluate their ideas or knowledge through the process of critical reflection (Moon, 2005). This approach contrasts with 'surface learning', where the student seeks to retain facts and information without testing or evaluating the information" (460). Rhem (1995) lists integration, intrinsic motivation, active learning, and interactions as the primary characteristics of deep learning. Bransford, Brown, and Cocking (2000) define deep learning as information that transfers from one setting to the next. Leamnson (2002) suggests that deep learning actually restructures the brain. Bacon and Stewart (2006) talk about deep learning in terms of students finding personal meaning.

Biggs and Tang (2007), also regarding both the student and teacher, state that a deep approach to teaching ensures a comprehensive grasp of the material by the student with meaningful engagement with the subject matter. Teachers will design their courses on the big picture, helping students understand underlying means and application of theory to practice. Students will become meaningfully engaged in the subject matter, much like a professor who is involved with research.

After examining previous research, Millis (2010) summarizes four basic characteristics of deep learning:

1. "A well-constructed knowledge base with a focus on concepts, integration of knowledge, and a cumulative experience."

2. "An appropriate motivational level, with an emphasis on intrinsic motivation and a sense of 'ownership' of the material."

3. "Learner activity associated with active, not passive, learning."

4. "Interaction with others, including student-teacher interactions and student-student interactions (Rhem, 1995, p.4; McCay amd Kember, 1997, p. 65)."

Millis (2010) concludes that deep learning requires teachers to identify fundamental and powerful concepts and then develop class activities that enable students to interact deeply with these concepts during class and outside of class. Teachers should design their courses to focus on key concepts, integrate knowledge, require a written product, create a sense on individual ownership, and encourage active student involvement with the material. This focus will help students understand, integrate, relate, and apply new knowledge to old learning. Further, "Deep learning leads to a genuine understanding that promotes long-term retention of the learned material and, just as important, the ability to retrieve it and apply it to new problems in unfamiliar concepts."

The years of research reveal several key principles involving the relationships among teachers, students, and learning: teaching in a way

*Deep learning leads to a genuine understanding that promotes long-term retention of the learned material and, just as important, the ability to retrieve it and apply it to new problems in unfamiliar concepts.*

that helps students learn deeply is important because students grasp powerful and fundamental concepts, transfer knowledge, and synthesize. They also enjoy learning, reflect on larger constructs, and apply skills by using multiple strategies to solve real world problems. Solidifying these findings, The American Institutes of Research (2014) lists six elements of knowledge, skill, and belief characteristic of student deeper learning:

- Mastery of Core Academic Content
- Critical Thinking and Problem Solving
- Collaboration
- Effective Communication
- Self-directed Learning, and
- An "Academic Mindset."

Summarizing extant research, Laird et al (2014) add to this list, suggesting some even more sweeping advantages: "Greater enjoyment of learning, reading widely, drawing on a variety of resources, discussing ideas with others, reflecting on how individual pieces of information relate to larger constructs or patterns, and applying knowledge in real world situations [Biggs, 2003; Entwhistle, 1981; Ramsden, 2003; Tagg, 2003]" (403). Laird, Shoup, & Kuh (2006) also add to this list, emphasizing "higher grades, and the ability to retain, integrate, and transfer information at higher rates, not to mention greater satisfaction with the learning experience." Ramsden (2003) goes so far as to claim deep learning as the fundamental basis of learning, "a qualitative change in a person's view of reality" (214).

# IMPLICATIONS

Obviously, the best learners are those who employ deep learning most often. Even the best learners, however, must be repeatedly instructed how to learn deeply so that eventually they develop effective deep learning strategies as well as deeply learning new knowledge. Rocconi, Ribera, and Laird (2014) sum up the research: "Compared to a surface approach, students who engage in DAL [Deep Approaches to Learning] are more likely to retain information for longer periods of time (Svensson 1977), earn better grades (Zeegers 2004; Zhang 2000), be more satisfied by the learning process (Tagg 2003), develop critical thinking skills (Chapman 2001), and integrate transfer information at higher rates (Prosser and Millar 1989)." As a value-added bonus, Rocconi, Ribera, and Laird (2014) also discovered that college students who use deep learning tend towards continuing their education in graduate school: "Findings revealed a significant positive relationship between seniors' use of DAL and plans for earning a graduate degree."

To help you understand the distinctions drawn in the research between these two learning approaches, we have created a table that summarizes the differences ("It was the best of approaches, it was the worst of approaches").

## A TALE OF TWO LEARNERS

|  | SURFACE LEARNERS | DEEP LEARNERS |
|---|---|---|
| APPROACH TOWARD IMPORTANCE | Fail to seek key concepts; tendency to think everything is equally important | Seek key concepts |
| SYNTHESIS | See each piece of knowledge as separate and unconnected—i.e., notice only the trees | Discover underlying patterns; engage in synthesis—i.e., see the individual trees as part of a forest |
| KEY STRATEGY | Memorize each new piece of knowledge as a distinct entity; often rely on mnemonics | Link new knowledge to old knowledge |
| MOTIVATION | Extrinsic, often for a good grade | Intrinsic |
| METACOGNITION | Exist in the moment, not aware of their awareness | Monitor their progress |
| CRITICAL THINKING | Tend not to utilize critical thinking | Evaluate their learning, especially the relationship between evidence and conclusions |
| ACTIVE/PASSIVE APPROACH | Become passive recipients of knowledge | Actively engage in the learning, usually by organizing the new knowledge |
| MINDSET | Tend to fall back on old knowledge and patterns—i.e., the easy path | Are intentional, coming to the new knowledge with a desire to master it—i.e., willing to take the complex path |
| ATTITUDE TOWARD ASSESSMENT | Clock in to do the work necessary to earn the degree | Love learning so much they transfer knowledge |
| COGNITIVE SILLS | Employ low-order cognitive skills | Employ high-order cognitive skills |

# REFERENCES

American Institutes of Research. (2014). *Deeper learning.* Retrieved from http://www.air.org/resources/deeper-learning

Bacon, D.R. and Stewart, K.A. (2006). How fast do students forget what they learn in consumer behavior? A longitudinal study. *Journal of Marketing Education, 28*, 181-192.

Bowden, J. and Marton, F. (1998). *The university of learning.* London: Kogan Page.

Bransford, J.D., Brown, A.L., & Cocking, R.R. (eds.) (2000). *How people learn: Brain, mind, experience, and school.* Commission on Behavioral and Social Sciences and Education National Research Council. Washington, DC: National Academy Press.

Biggs, J.B., and C. Tang. (2007). *Teaching for quality learning at university*, (3rd ed). Berkshire: Open University Press.

Drummer, T., Cook, I., Parker, S. Barrett, G., & Hull, A. (2008) Promoting and assessing 'deep learning' in geography fieldwork: An evaluation of reflective field diaries. *Journal of Geography in Higher Education, 32*(3), 459-479.

Entwistle, N. (1988). *Styles of learning and teaching.* London: David Fulton.

Laird, T., Shoup, R., & Kuh, G. (2006, May). *Measuring deep approaches to learning using the national survey of student engagement.* Presentation at the annual meeting of the Association for Institutional Research, Chicago, Il.

Laird, T., Seifert, T., Pascarella, E., Mayhew, M. & Blaich, C. (2014). Deeply affecting first-year students' thinking: Deep approaches to learning and three dimensions of cognitive development. *Journal of Higher Education, 85*(3), 402-432.

Leamnson, R. (2002). *Learning (Your first job).* Retrieved November 14th, 2015 from http://www.ctl.uga.edu/Learning/.

Marton, F. & Saljo.R. (1976). On qualitative differences in learning: Outcome and process. *British Journal of Educational Psychology, 46*, 4-11.

McDrury, J., and Alterio, M. (2004). *Learning through story telling in higher education. Using reflection and experience to improve learning.* Sterling, VA: Dunmore Press.

Millis, B.J., (2010) Promoting Deep Learning, Idea Paper number 47, University of Texas, The Idea Center. Retrieved November 12th 2015 from http:/www.theideacenter.org/IDEAPaper47.

Millis, B. J., (2014). Using cooperative structures to promote deep learning. *Journal on Excellence in College Teaching, 25*(3&4), 139-148.

Ramsden, P. (2003). *Learning to teach in higher education.* 2nd ed. London, UK: Routledge.

Rhem, J. (2009-10). Deep/surface approaches to learning in higher education: A research update. In *Essays on Teaching Excellence: Toward the Best in the Academy, 21*(8).

Rocconi, L., Ribera. A., & Laird, T. (2014, November). College seniors' plans for graduate school: Do deep approaches to learning and Holland academic environments matter? *Research in Higher Education.* DOI: 10.1007/s11162-014-9358-3.

Sweet, C., Blythe, H. Phillips, B., & Daniels C. (2014). *Achieving excellence in teaching.* Stillwater: New Forums Press.

Tagg, J. (2003). *The learning paradigm college.* San Francisco, CA: Jossey-Bass.

# 3. The Making of Academic Surfers: Characteristics of Today's College Students and Culture That Hinder Deep Learning

**LEARNING QUIZ** (True or False)

1. Rereading is an effective strategy for deeply learning new material.

2. More than half of all incoming first-year students report studying more than six hours per week in high school.

3. The average first-year college student reads at the 9$^{th}$-grade reading level.

4. The Internet inculcates deep learning skills in students.

5. Just as pressure builds diamonds, stress promotes deep learning.

## BACKGROUND

> *Bellignorance is the willful and active resistance to new knowledge because old knowledge contradicts it.*

A few years ago in our classes we all ran into a similar scenario. Whether we were trying to teach the basic organization of an essay or an in-depth analysis of T. S. Eliot's "The Love Song of J. Alfred Prufrock," some students always resisted our attempts at instruction. When confronted with new knowledge, they would eventually tell us to our face or write us a note/email to the effect of "That's not what I learned in high school." After confronting this scenario a number of times, we finally created a name for the phenomenon—**bellignorance**.

Bellignorance is <u>the willful and active resistance to new knowledge because old knowledge contradicts it</u>. Ideally, new knowledge is built on old, but too often our students' old knowledge didn't act like a Lego block on which to snap some new awareness; rather, it functioned as a stone wall preventing the adoption of new knowledge. From where, we wondered, did this bellignorance arise. The answer, we believe, is complex.

Not only have academic forces encouraged today's higher education students to swim mainly in shallow pools, but also the pop universe in which these students dwell has stunted their growth, turning them into academic surfers. Often, the very things that seemed their friends in high school turn into postsecondary enemies, but they have become habits, usually unconscious ones, that are as hard to break up with as the guy or girl back home.

## ACADEMIC IMPEDIMENTS

**Poor Study Habits**. Ever ask a student how s/he studied for your test? "Oh, I reread all the assigned material." Others will tell you that they believe in the underlining method to emphasize important points, but when you look at their notes, you find nearly every word underlined. Some have narrative paragraphs with quote marks around various phrases to indicate you told them those very words in class. By far, the most common response is, "I had a cram session last night from 9:00-11:00." Of course, they studied alone, the ballgame was on in the background, and numerous friends called or dropped by. Why have they taken this one or a combination of these approaches? Most likely, they were taught the strategies, and through repetition they honed them into bad habits. How they studied in high school seems to be the main determinant for their collegiate study habits.

Addressing one of the major deterrents to learning in college, a Cal Poly message to entering students explains the discrepancy between high school study time and that in college as follows: "In high school, you were in class 35 hours a week and did about five hours of homework for a total of 40 hours per week. In college, you will only be in class 15-20 hours per week, and college is more challenging than high school. You will need to do a lot more learning on your own. To succeed at Cal Poly, you will need to study two hours per unit per week, or 25-35 hours per week. That's 40-50 total hours per week, which is similar to high school and the equivalent of a full-time job." The Higher Education Research Institute (2013) studied a broad range of postsecondary institutions, and almost 60% of incoming students reported studying fewer than six hours per week. Do college students actually get the message of the need for more studying? A recent National Survey of Student Engagement (NSSE) study of Eastern Kentucky University seniors found them self-reporting only five hours per week—exactly the same number Cal Poly found high school students studying outside the classroom.

In sum, what students possess are poor study habits, when what they need are effective learning strategies.

**Deleterious Testing Effect**. By the time students reach college, they have been subjected to a barrage of testing, both high (e.g., national, state, or local test) and low stakes. The No Child Left Behind Act of 2001 mandates that states test children 17 times before high school graduation. In Pittsburgh, for example, students take 20-25, or more, high-stakes tests a year, with new tests added in 2015 in art and music. In a policy statement, the National Council of Teachers of English (NCTE) cited a study that "teachers lose between 60 to 110 hours of instructional time in a year because of testing [preparation and follow-up] and the institutional tests that surround it." One wonders how much total time is being devoted to testing. Alarmed by this trend, the federal government that created the high-stakes testing situation now recommends that "states cap the percentage of time students spend taking required state assessments at 2 percent."

What are the effects on students of all this testing and ancillary activity around testing? Yeh (2005) identifies four negative classroom effects produced by such requirements:

- "Narrowing the curriculum by excluding from it subject matter not tested.

- Excluding topics either not tested or not likely to appear on the test even within tested subjects.

- Reduced learning to the memorization of facts easily recalled for multiple-choice testing.

- Devoting too much classroom time to test preparation rather than learning."

After investigating this vital area, *Washington Post* reporter Valerie Strauss (2014) also listed some deleterious effects of the over-devotion to testing, among them being "lost learning time . . . Reduced content knowledge . . . Narrowed curriculum. . . Loss of curiosity and love of learning."

To these harmful effects we'd like to add one more. If students are repeatedly shown that these important tests are answered by bubbling in a multiple-choice question, they are being conditioned to believe that all the important questions in life have single answers and are consequently left with a less than complex view of the world. College, on the other hand, demands critical thinking, evaluating arguments, and eventually realizing that various disciplines produce shades of gray, not black and white choices. While 2 + 2=4 and Ohm's Law are constants, Wallace Stevens showed us "Thirteen Ways of Looking at a Blackbird," and Voltaire's Candide effectively questioned the optimist's view of the world. As moot court teams have demonstrated, since absolutes seldom exist in the real world, often the winning claim is the one that has the most effective evidence to bolster it.

Tragically, high school students are not being equipped to deal with post-secondary's methodology for constructing knowledge.

**Inadequate Reading Skills**. When Charlie began teaching in college, he used a 2250-page volume called *World Literature*, which meant his

*Tragically, high school students are not being equipped to deal with post-secondary's methodology for constructing knowledge.*

students had to read about 60 pages of it to prepare for each class. Thirty years later he had cut the reading assignments for the same class down to 12 pages per night. Why? He discovered that his students could not or would not (he couldn't tell the difference) read the large number of pages, so he made a compact with them: I'll give you a smaller assignment to digest, and you will read all the material thoroughly (of course, he gave daily quizzes as insurance). What Charlie didn't know was, as reading expert Sandra Stotsky clarifies, "most college textbooks and adult literary works written before 1970 require mature reading skills." Unfortunately, Charlie began teaching in 1970, and over the years his students became less able (and, perhaps, willing) to confront the lengthy, complex assignments.

Simply put, we are smack dab in the middle of a literacy crisis. Today's college students are reading at the lowest level since literacy tests were first given, and if college professors want these students to read complex works, they may as well try to touch them with Harry Potter's wand (the good news is that most entering collegians will catch that allusion). Stated another way, college students can't read what they need to read in the effective manner necessary.

Overstatement, you say. Do college students read at the 13th-grade or even 16th-grade level by the time they become seniors. Renaissance Learning examined the summer reading books assigned by colleges, and according to Beach Books: 2013-2014, the reading level for the top five to seven books was 7.56 (i.e., grade 7, sixth month). If we drill down deeper, claims Stotsky (2015), we discover the average entering first-year reading level is 6.8: "colleges are not demanding a college-level reading experience for incoming freshmen." Ah, argue supporters, Common Core will make things better, but Stotsky says, "Common Core's reading `standards' are, for the most part, empty skill sets. Moreover, there is nothing in its English language/arts/reading document to indicate that students are to be assigned and taught to read more difficult material than they are already reading— grade after grade—in a coherent reading curriculum." If the Common Core curriculum, intended to raise the level of achievement of America's students, offers little or no change, the picture is indeed bleak.

And getting bleaker. The findings of Renaissance Learning are confirmed by a 2005 study wherein the ACT tested high school graduates. According to their Executive Summary, "it appears that only about half of our nation's ACT-tested high school students are ready for college-level reading. What's worse, more students are on track to being ready for college-level reading in eighth and tenth grade than are actually ready by the time they reach twelfth grade." In other words, the K-12 school system not only fails to prepare students for postsecondary work, but high schools actually impede reading progress.

Consider other implications of this failure to advance reading proficiency. As Stotsky emphasizes, "Low literacy levels often prevent students from mastering other subjects." But colleges seem either to ignore or to

*In other words, the K-12 school system not only fails to prepare students for postsecondary work, but high schools actually impede reading progress.*

be unable to correct the problem. With students reading at about half the grade level they should, only "Eleven percent of entering postsecondary school students are enrolled in remedial reading coursework," and "Seventy percent of students who took one or more remedial reading courses do not attain a college degree with eight years of enrollment."

In 2006 The National Survey of America's College Students examined the same group's reading skills, finding, "More than 50% of students at four-year schools and more than 75% of two-year colleges lacked the skills to perform complex literacy tasks." Furthermore, the report concluded, "The average literacy of U.S. college students was generally the same regardless of how long students had been in college." Shockingly, they seemingly learn little . . . or nothing.

In 2012 a damning report from the College Board came out that explained this failure to progress: "The vast majority of the nation's 2012 high school graduates aren't ready for college, and SAT reading scores have plummeted to their lowest level in four decades, new data show. . . . Fifty-seven percent failed to clear the test's 1550-point college and career readiness benchmark."

Just when you think student readiness for reading has bottomed out, along comes more contemporary evidence. A report in the 28 October 2015 *The Wall Street Journal* announces, "Reading scores were roughly flat for fourth-graders and down for eighth-graders. . . . In eighth grade, 34% were proficient or better, down two percentage points" from the previous year.

In short, despite all the money and effort thrown at the situation, Johnny and Joanna still can't read, they are worse in terms of literacy than their parents, and the picture grows darker for their children.

**Technology Is Not the Savior**. The advent of the Internet, ever-better hardware, and new software have generally been greeted with a halo effect. More students have access to education, programming can aid individual learners, and students feel so positive about what technology offers them. Pearson Allyn Bacon Prentice Hall representatives O'Hara and Pritchard (2014) glowingly report, "Research literature throughout the past decade has shown that technology can enhance literacy development, impact language acquisition, provide greater access to information, support learning, motivate students, and enhance self-esteem." Other research demonstrates students possess increased technical skills (sometimes even greater than that of the teacher), they work cooperatively, they can provide peer tutoring, and their design skills have improved (http://www2.ed.gov/pubs/EdReformStudies/EdTech/effectsstudents.html).

On the other hand, some researchers feel compelled to stress the negative effects of what we called in *Teaching Applied Creative Thinking* (2013), a "Techtonic Shift in the Role of Technology" (29). Deloach (2015) lists "The Four Negative Sides of Technology." For our purposes, her most important point is Negative #1: "Technology Changes the Way Children Think": media usage "can lead to distraction and deceased memory. Children who always use search engines may become very good at finding information—but not very good at remembering it. . . . children who use too much technology may not have enough opportunities to use their imagination or to read and think deeply about the material." According to Richtel (2012), a Pew Survey (2012) performed in conjunction with the College Board and the National Writing Project, while noting that the Internet and search engines had a "mostly positive" impact on student research skills, also enumerated two major problems:

- An easily distracted generation with short attention spans

- The Wikipedia Problem: students who become accustomed to obtaining quick answers with a few key strokes are more likely to give up on more complex answers.

Perhaps the best analysis of technology's harmful effects can be found in Carr's *The Shallows* (2010). According to Carr's assessment of the research, the Internet works against deep thinking and creativity: "There is no Sleepy Hollow on the Internet, no peaceful spot where contemplativeness can work its restorative magic. . . . It's not only deep thinking that requires a calm, attentive mind. It's also empathy and compassion" (220). How does the Internet transform its users into what playwright Richard Foreman refers to as "pancake people—spread wide and thin as we connect with that vast network of information accessed by the mere touch of a button" (Carr, 196)? In 2009 research revealed teens sending over 70 texts per day and "eight and a half hours per day looking at a television, a computer monitor, or the screen of a mobile phone," but only 7 minutes a day were spent reading printed texts (86-87). Furthermore, researchers have found Americans have developed a click mentality, reading less than one-fifth of an Internet page and spending less than ten seconds on that page (134-135). Google distracts—Twitter becomes like an addictive drug.

What's the result? Attracted to these rapidly changing bright stimuli of Surf City (with apologies to Jan and Dean), **students have become skimmers, riding their virtual boards over the surface of information, rarely pausing to create or think deeply**, but rarely do we see the DANGER, SURF'S UP signs.

## NON-ACADEMIC IMPEDIMENTS

**Negative Learning States**. As reported in *USA Today*, a recent survey (2015) of 22,000 U.S. high school students by the Born This Way Foundation asked for their emotional disposition and discovered that eight of the top ten responses were negative, with the top three being "tired," "stressed," and "bored." Obviously, such negative emotional states deter deep learning.

*Furthermore, researchers have found Americans have developed a click mentality, reading less than one-fifth of an Internet page and spending less than ten seconds on that page.*

Fear of Missing Out (**FOMO**)—technically athazagoraphobia—is being recognized as a driver in young adults. Such people believe they must be connected—most often through their cellphone—to the world around them. Teachers who have attempted to take away their phones have found real anxiety developing.

**Standardized testing** can cause stress in students, claims Scott Paris, a professor of psychology at the University of Michigan. As a result, reports Daniel Edelstein, students may exhibit "disturbed sleep patterns, tiredness, worry, irregular eating habit, increased infections, and inability to concentrate." Decreased memory capacity may also occur. And as Frodl and O'Keane (2013) summarize the problem, "There is evidence that excessive stress exposure of the brain, mediated through the neurotoxic effects of cortisol and possibly neuroinflammation, causes damage to brain structure and function" (25).

In *Brain Rules* (2008), Medina's eighth rule is "Stressed brains don't learn the same way" (169). After explaining that stress accounts for 80% of our medical expenditures, Medina focuses on its detrimental cognitive effects, especially to the business world: "Prolonged stress can cause depression, which alters the ability to think—a direct assault on a corporation's intellectual capital. . . . Fluid intelligence, problem-solving abilities (including quantitative reasoning), and memory formation are deeply affected by depression. The result is an erosion of innovation and creativity" (186-187).

Teachers looking out into the classroom need also to see packages labelled FRAGILE—HANDLE CAREFULLY!

**Cultural Soundbite Mentality.** Years ago when *USA Today* started up, the editors felt they could deliver any news story in seven paragraphs. Ted Turner started CNN, and in order to make news easier to digest, he came up with HLN, Headline News that simplifies the broad spectrum of news by focusing on a few stories. As Mohammed el-Nawawy puts it, "There is a tendency in most mainstream American news media to adopt a superficial 'soundbite culture' that neglects the context of critical events and focuses on filling the 24-hour news hole. . . . The shallow coverage and the speed with which news disappears from the headlines means that important events don't get the debate and reflection they deserve."

When television first started, TV commercials lasted sixty seconds. Three decades ago the thirty-second commercial became the industry standard. In the late 80s, fifteen-second commercials began to appear. By 2005, according to Stuart Elliot, an analysis by Media IQ found "15-second spots account for more than 36 percent of all commercial time sold by the major broadcast networks." Is it any wonder students spend almost exactly that amount of time on a website?

Today's college students, then, were raised on fifteen-second sound bites—and the tube. Carr cites a 2009 study by Ball State University's

Center for Media Design that finds, "most Americans, no matter what their age, spend at least eight and a half hours a day looking at a television, a computer monitor, or the screen of their mobile phone" (87).

When students transfer that short, simplistic learning experience to the classroom, what kind of mental processes should we expect?

***Jeopardy* Mindset**. In 2004 Ken Jennings won 74 consecutive *Jeopardy* games and became an instant cultural icon. His subsequent books and appearances on the *Jeopardy* "Ultimate Tournament of Champions" and *Are You Smarter Than a 5th Grader?* cemented our perception of what we consider intelligence in America—we revere the person who dominates the lower levels of Bloom's taxonomy of learning, remembering and understanding.

Orlin (2013) defines memorization as "learning an isolated fact through deliberate effort." To prepare for tests, students are taught raw rehearsal (reciting the fact over and over) and mnemonics (artificial tricks, such as HOMES being the way to recall the Great Lakes). But, as Orlin says, "Such tactics . . . don't solve the underlying problem: They still bypass real conceptual learning."

Factual knowledge is necessary, even if your goal is not to thrive on *Jeopardy*, but memorizing factoids is only the first step in climbing up Bloom's Taxonomy. Too often such information is forgotten long before Final Jeopardy. The most troubling problem is that learning frequently seems to stop there. Darling-Hammond (2011), one of the experts called by the National Research Council (2011) to identify the competencies that lead to deeper learning skills, believes, as reported by Towler (2014), "the focus on memorization, fueled by standardized testing, has obstructed learning."

*Too often such information is forgotten long before Final Jeopardy.*

Ultimately, as Scouller (1998) reports, "Research on learning in higher education suggests that students have a preferred approach to their studies, usually referred to as either a deep approach (focusing on meaning and understanding) or a surface approach (focusing on recall and reproduction)" (453). Unfortunately, even pop culture reinforces for college students the worse tendencies of the K-12 classroom, resulting in a surface or shallow approach to learning.

# REFERENCES

ACT. (2006). Executive Summary. In *Reading between the lines: What the ACT reveals about college readiness in reading*. Retrieved from https://www.act.org/research/policymakers/pdf/reading_summary.pdf

Associated Press. (2006, January 20). *Reports on college literacy level sobering*. Retrieved from http://www.nbcnews.com/id/10928755/ns/us_news-education/t/reports-college-literacy-levels-sobering/#.VjoNDLerTcs

Baer, J. D., Cook, A. L., Baldi, S. (2006). Executive Summary. In *The literacy of America's college students*. Retrieved from http://www.air.org/sites/default/files/downloads/report/The20Literacy20of20Americas_20College20Students_final20report_0.pdf

Brody, L. (2015, October 28). Pupils' test scores slip. *The Wall Street Journal,* pp. A3.

Cal Poly. (n.d.). *Supporting student success.* Retrieved from http://www.cosam.calpoly.edu/content/student_success

Camera, L. (2015, October 24). *Education department recommends less testing.* Retrieved from http://www.usnews.com/news/articles/2015/10/24/education-department-recommends-less-testing

Carr, N. (2010). *The shallows.* New York, NY: W. W. Norton & Company, Inc.

Center for Public Education. (2006, March 30). Retrieved from http://www.centerforpubliceducation.org/Main-Menu/Instruction/High-stakes-testing-and-effects-on-instruction-At-a-glance/High-stakes-testing-and-effects-on-instruction-Research-review.html

Dartmouth College. (n. d.). *Active reading: Comprehension and rate.* Retrieved from http://www.dartmouth.edu/~acskills/success/reading.html

DeLoatch, P. (2015, May 2). *The four negative sides of technology.* Retrieved from http://www.edudemic.com/the-4-negative-side-effects-of-technology/

Edelstein, D. (2000, July 12). *Tests + stress = problems for students.* Retrieved from http://brainconnection.brainhq.com/2000/07/12/tests-stress-problems-for-students/

El-Nawawy, M. (2012, September 19). *The news media and its 'soundbite culture.'* Retrieved from http://www.nytimes.com/roomfordebate/2012/09/18/just-the-scandal-of-the-week-or-a-turning-point/the-news-media-and-its-soundbite-culture

Frodl, T. & O'Keane, V. (2013). How does the brain deal with cumulative stress? A review with focus on development stress, HPA axis function and hippocampal structure in humans. *Neurobiology of Disease, 52,* 24-37. Doi: 10.1016.j.nbd.2012.03.012

Hope, M. (2015, January 3). *Expert: Most US college freshmen read at 7th grade level.* Retrieved from http://www.breitbart.com/texas/2015/01/03/expert-most-us-college-freshmen-read-at-7th-grade-level/

Johnson, J. (2013, September 14). Today's typical college students often juggle work, children and bills with coursework. Retrieved from https://www.washingtonpost.com/local/education/todays-typical-college-students-often-juggle-work-children-and-bills-with-coursework/2013/09/14/4158c8c0-1718-11e3-804b-d3a1a3a18f2c_story.html

Ken Jennings. (n.d.). Retrieved November 3, 2015 from https://en.m.wikipedia.org/wiki/Ken_Jennings

Landor-Ngemi, J. (2007, October 9). *What are the characteristics of today's students? In what way do they differ from the traditional students?* Retrieved from http://jarrettlandor.blogspot.com/2007/10/what-are-characteristics-of-todays.html

Lit, M. (2015, January 6). The average college freshman reads at 7th grade level. Retrieved from http://campusreform.org/?ID=6174

Lytle, R. (2011, July 14). Study: Emerging technology has positive impact in classroom. Retrieved from http://www.usnews.com/education/high-schools/articles/2011/07/14/study-emerging-technology-has-positive-impact-in-classroom

Medina, J. (2008). *Brain rules.* Seattle, WA: Pear Press.

National Center for Education Statistics. (2015, May). *Characteristics of postsecondary students*. Retrieved from http://nces.ed.gov/programs/coe/indicator_csb.asp

National Council of Teachers of English. (2014). How standardized tests shape — and limit — student learning. Retrieved from http://www.ncte.org/library/NCTEFiles/Resources/Journals/CC/0242-nov2014/CC0242PolicyStandardized.pdf

O'Hara, S. & Pritchard, R. (2014, April 30). *What is the impact of technology on learning*? Retrieved from http://www.education.com/reference/article/what-impact-technology-learning/

Orlin, B. (2013, September 9). When memorization gets in the way of learning. Retrieved from http://www.theatlantic.com/education/archive/2013/09/when-memorization-gets-in-the-way-of-learning/279425/

Richtel, M. (2012, November 1). *Technology changing how students learn, teachers say*. Retrieved from http://nyti.msW8Zv7M

Schmid, R. F., Bernard, R. M., Borokhovski, E., Tamim, R., Abrami, P. C., Wade, C. A., Surkes, M. A., & Lowerison, G. (2009). Technology's effect on achievement in higher education: a Stage I meta-analysis of classroom applications. *Journal of Computing in Higher Education, 21*(2), 95-109. Doi: 10.1007/s12528-009-9021-8

Scouller, K. (1998). The influence of assessment method on students' learning approaches: Multiple choice question examination versus assignment essay. *Higher Education, 35,* 453-472.

Stotsky, S. (2015, January 9). *Why no information on what a college-readiness reading level is*? Retrieved from http://www.educationviews.org/information-college-readiness-reading-level-is/

Strauss, V. (2014, March 11). *13 ways high-stakes standardized tests hurt students*. Retrieved from https://www.washingtonpost.com/news/answer-sheet/wp/2014/03/10/13-ways-high-stakes-standardized-tests-hurt-students/

Toppo, G. (2015, October 23). Survey finds high school kids tired, bored. *USA Today,* pp. A1.

Towler, L. (2014, November 25*). Deeper learning: Moving students beyond memorization.* Retrieved from http://neatoday.org/2014/11/25/deeper-learning-moving-students-beyond-memorization-2/

U.S. Department of Education. (n.d.). Archived: Effects of technology on classrooms and students. Retrieved from https://www2.ed.gov/pubs/EdReformStudies/EdTech/effectsstudents.html

Wolfgang, B. (2012, September 24). *Data: High school students aren't ready for college.* Retrieved from http://www.washingtontimes.com/news/2012/sep/24/high-school-grads-reading-skills-hit-new-low-most-/print/v

# 4. The Learning Gap

Back in those thrilling days of yesteryear when Hal, Bill, and Charlie were kids (Rusty's dad had just married the schoolmarm), they were thrilled by TV and movie westerns that so dominated pop culture. Somewhere in those classic adventures a stock scene recurred in which the hero, be it the Cisco Kid, Zorro, or the Lone Ranger, while being chased or needing to take a shortcut to thwart the bad guys, came to a chasm/abyss/arroyo. At that point the hero depended on Diablo, Tornado, or Silver as the answer to his plight.

Well, pardners, if you've been reading the preceding chapters in order, you recognize both the existence of a gap in the educational landscape and that we in higher education need more than a trusty steed to span it. Both academic and cultural research tell us that the students entering our institutions are coming to us not only underprepared but also conditioned by their K-12 experience as well as their cultural environment to entertain certain expectations. Unfortunately, both for them and us, these expectations run counter to cognitive processes required for success in college.

When Hal and Charlie became co-directors of Eastern Kentucky University's Teaching & Learning Center (TLC), they developed a motto that they believed captured the essence of the TLC's mission: Helping Teachers Help Students Learn. For the first few years, the motto served them well, but as they continued to work with faculty and engage in pedagogical research, they realized that while helping students learn was commendable, it was not enough. Indeed, everyone from professional developers such as Dee Fink and Saundra McGuire to brain scientists such as John Medina was calling for faculty to strive for a more lasting form of learning in their students, a learning that would transcend the boundaries of disciplines—a deeper learning. As a result, Charlie and Hal revised the TLC's motto to reflect this new goal of "Helping Teachers Help Students Learn **Deeply**."

Go back and look at the chart at the end of Chapter 2. When you read that section earlier, you doubtlessly noticed the large amount of white space between the two columns labelled "Deep Learning" and "Surface Learning." Did you ask yourself why the space was there, or did you simply figure the four of us were terrible proofreaders?

Obviously, that space is intentional, and it represents what we've deemed **The Learning Gap**. Our initial research and teaching led the four of us to start giving more serious thought to just what constitutes the learning gap that hinders faculty in moving students from where they are to where they need to be. After even more research and discussion with colleagues, we realized that the gap between surface and deep learning involved several factors and that teachers could employ certain strategies to aid students in leaping the perilous chasm.

The following eight chapters will cover our **EIGHT EXCELLENT STRATEGIES FOR DEEP LEARNING** as well as the **Basic Rubric for Improving Deep Learning Enhancement (BRIDLE)**, a self-help rubric for implementing the "Excellent Eight." The rubric appears at the end of each of the succeeding eight chapters for readers to assess their own skills as well as in its complete version in Chapter 14. :

- Chapter 5 focuses on "Climbing Bloom's Staircase toward Deep Learning."
- Chapter 6 explains "Presenting for Deep Learning."
- Chapter 7 explores "Facilitating Retrieving for Deep Learning."
- Chapter 8 covers "Fostering Metacognition for Deep Learning."
- Chapter 9 treats "Developing Critical Thinking for Deep Learning."
- Chapter 10 examines "Employing Deep Reading for Deep Learning."
- Chapter 11 investigates "Creating Spaces for Deep Learning."
- Chapter 12 deals with "Motivating Your Students to be Deep Learners."

Just as the construction industry uses Laminated Veneer Lumber (LVL), an engineered wood product made from many layers of thin wood strips glued together for strength, so our bridge across the learning gap has a similar composition of melded strategies. While any one of these eight strategies by itself might provide a skinny, precarious rope bridge like the one in *Indiana Jones and the Temple of Doom*, the most effective and most solid bridge is constructed by combining our chapter topics.

Each of the chapters will make liberal use of academic, cultural, and brain research while striving to remain as "user friendly" as possible. Now, get ready to pull your students up on the horse's back and navigate across the learning gap as you help transform them into deep learners. And you've got something Zorro never had—a bridge.

> *While any one of these eight strategies by itself might provide a skinny, precarious rope bridge like the one in* Indiana Jones and the Temple of Doom, *the most effective and most solid bridge is constructed by combining our chapter topics.*

# Part II

## Eight Excellent Strategies for Deep Learning: Using Bridle

# 5. STRATEGY I: Climbing Bloom's Staircase

**LEARNING QUIZ** (True or False)

1. Whether you teach Bloom's Taxonomy intentionally or unintentionally doesn't matter.

2. Bloom's Taxonomy, created way back in 1956, has never been revised.

3. In 1956 Bloom used a series of active verbs to suggest a dynamic conception of classification.

4. Successful college students focus primarily on Bloom's lower-order thinking skills.

5. Introducing Bloom's Taxonomy at the beginning of a semester is all an instructor has to do to ensure deep learning.

# BACKGROUND

The first twenty-five years or so Hal and Charlie taught in higher education, they, having never taken an education course or been part of a faculty development program, had never heard of Bloom's Taxonomy. Nevertheless, in their World Lit and American Lit classes, they constructed tests with a three-part format:

1. **Fill-in-the-blank questions**. Here students merely had to recall key information/concepts (e.g., 1. _____ is Hemingway's theory of fiction writing that writers may omit a key central piece of information around which the story revolves if they know they are doing so.).

2. **Short Paragraphs**. Here students were required to perform basic tasks, such as comparing and contrasting, applying a concept discussed in one poem to a poem never discussed, or analyzing the major themes/images in work excerpts (e.g., Discuss how Faulkner's imagery in the opening paragraph of "Barn Burning" foreshadows major plot threads.).

3. **Essay Questions**. Here students were asked to spend about half the test utilizing information. One essay might call on them to imagine a

scene between a story's two major protagonists, while another might ask them to analyze one verse of a poem to determine if it reflected Romantic or Neoclassic values or both.

In retrospect, what Hal and Charlie were doing was within each testing situation pushing their students up Bloom's Taxonomy, starting with fill-ins that demanded remembering and understanding, through applying, and into analyzing, evaluating, and creating. The problem is that while they may have intuited a hierarchical progression of learning levels that was helping their students move from lower-order to developing higher-order cognitive skills, neither they nor their students were conscious of that process. From both a teaching and a learning perspective, instructors and students must become conscious of what they are doing and why — i.e., using Bloom's Taxonomy must be an **intentional** act.

But we get ahead of ourselves. Many students and college instructors today are like Hal and Charlie were back then—unaware of what Bloom's Taxonomy is and its significance—so let's back up and offer a basic primer.

In 1956 Benjamin Bloom and four collaborators — all educational psychologists--published their *Taxonomy of Educational Objectives*, a framework of educational goals that became known in popular educational parlance as Bloom's Taxonomy. Although his group developed three domains—the cognitive (knowledge-based), the affective (heart-based feelings), and the psychomotor (action-based), the most-used and most-remembered domain is the cognitive. Knowledge--"the recall of specifics and universals, the recall of methods and processes, or the recall of a pattern, structure or setting" (p. 201) — was seen as the necessary foundation for putting these "skills and abilities" into practice. Forty-five years later, Krathwohl, an original collaborator, and Anderson, a Bloom student, revised the famed pyramid in *A Taxonomy for Learning, Teaching, and Assessing: A Revision of Bloom's Taxonomy of Educational Objectives* (2001). Responding to the idea that the original "educational objectives" might be too static, they developed a more dynamic taxonomy as emphasized by their use of verbs and gerunds rather than nouns.

In truth, Bloom and company discussed three domains—the cognitive, affective, and psychomotor—but in keeping with our KISS principle in writing this book, we're emphasizing only the first.

> *From both a teaching and a learning perspective, instructors and students must become conscious of what they are doing and why – i.e., using Bloom's Taxonomy must be an **intentional** act.*

Here is a juxtaposition of the two pyramids:

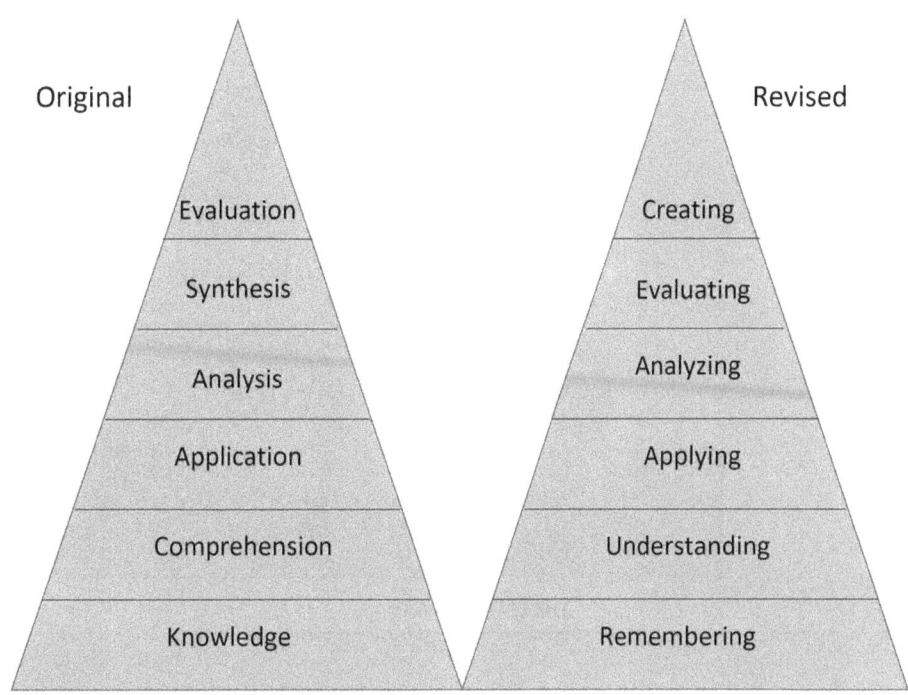

**Figure 5.1 and Figure 5.2**

Traditionally, the bottom two levels have been thought of as lower-order cognitive skills, while the top four constitute higher-order thinking. While a hierarchy definitely exists between lower-order and higher-order skills, critics debate whether the four higher-order skills constitute a hierarchy in themselves or are in fact parallel. In our way of thinking the last point remains moot as other than for artificial assignments a multiplicity of higher-order skills is needed. With one caveat. All of our research for *Introduction to Applied Creative Thinking* (2012) and *Teaching Applied Creative Thinking* (2013) as well as our experiences in teaching and writing (both fiction and non-fiction) has demonstrated to us sufficiently that creating is the most difficult skill for teachers and students to master.

To illustrate the hierarchal nature of the revised Bloom as well as the need to move students from lower-order thinking skills to higher-order ones, we offer still another version of the famed taxonomy that we call Bloom's Staircase.

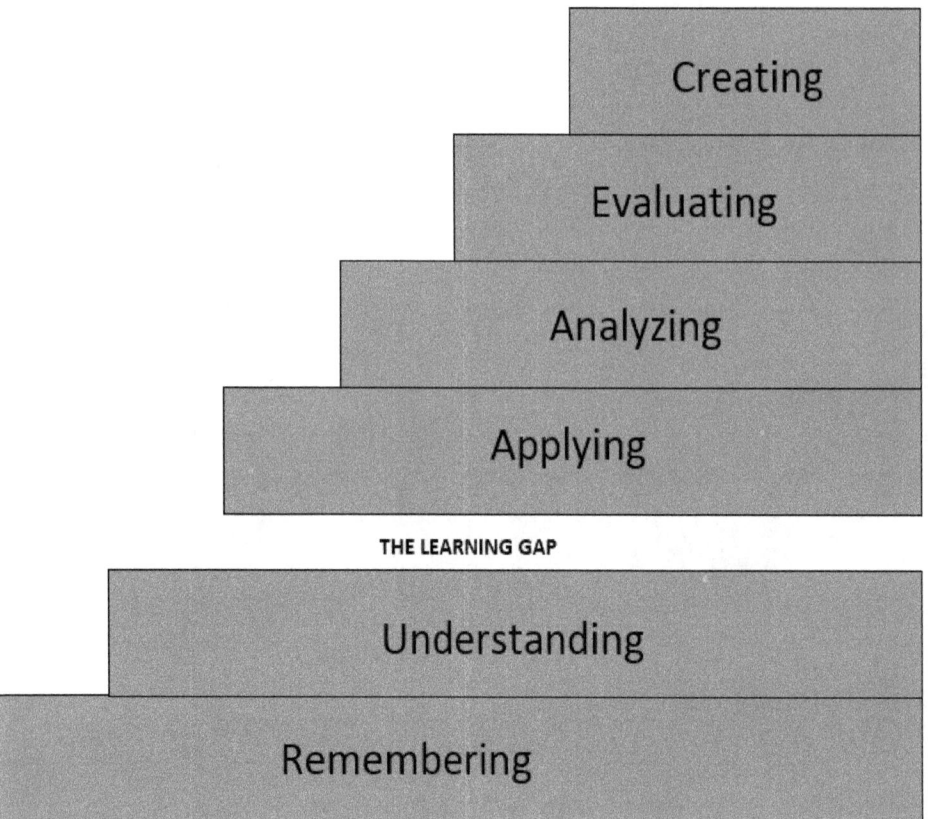

**Figure 5.3**

Research finds that Hal and Charlie's aforementioned lack of knowledge about Bloom in postsecondary pedagogy is not unusual. According to Crowe, Dirks, and Wenderoth (2008), "Bloom has been used widely since the 1960s in K-12 education (Kunene et al, 1981; Imrie, 1995) but has seen only limited application in selected disciplines in higher education (Demetrulias and McCubbin, 1982; Ball and Washburn, 2001; Taylor et al, 2002; Athanassiou *et al*, 2003)" (369). Obviously, the best college teachers should guide their students up Bloom's staircase. As Cook, Kennedy, and McGuire stress, "Most students experience difficulty because they are focused on memorizing facts and formulas instead of understanding concepts and developing problem-solving skills. However, students can be successful if they are taught how to shift their efforts from low-level to higher-order thinking" (961). McGuire (2015) elaborates on the importance of Bloom in closing the learning gap: "When students understand the different levels in Bloom's, they can immediately see the difference between the kind of work required of them in high school and the work they need to do in college" (30). Sure, higher-order thinking is more difficult, but to quote Tom Hanks in *A League of Their Own* (1992), "The hard is what makes it great."

> *Obviously, the best college teachers should guide their students up Bloom's staircase.*

# TACTICS FOR USING BLOOM IN YOUR CLASSES

If Bloom's Taxonomy is deemed so important, how can higher education teachers incorporate it into their instruction?

1. **Start by using Bloom's language in your student learning outcomes (SLOs)**. Bloom will provide you with a valuable focus, helping you and your students move from lower-order to the higher-order skills (sometimes called "Spiraling"). For example:

- **Remembering**: Students will be able to recall the definitions of the course's most fundamental and powerful concepts.

- **Understanding**: Students will be able to interpret — i.e., paraphrase in their own words — the course's most fundamental and powerful concepts.

- **Applying**: Students will be able to apply the course's most fundamental and powerful concepts to materials not covered in the course content.

- **Analyzing**: Students will be able to analyze materials in order to discover the course's fundamental and powerful concepts.

- **Evaluating**: Students will be able to judge materials using the course's most fundamental and powerful concepts.

- **Creating**: Students will be able to develop a product (i.e., piece of art, video, PowerPoint innovation, new idea) that comes out of their understanding of the course's most fundamental and powerful concepts.

Using the Bloom approach to SLOs obviously depends on your discipline for specificity.

2. **Early in the semester provide a short introduction to Bloom's Taxonomy to your students**. You might include the Bloom's Taxonomy on your syllabus, or you might simply place it in your course-management system (e.g., Blackboard), but do more than just mention it in passing. The Bloom's Taxonomy icon is a powerful learning tool, for as Medina reminds us in *Brain Rules* (2008), Rule #10 is "Vision trumps all other senses. . . . If information is presented orally, people remember about 10 percent, tested 72 hours after exposure. That figure goes up to 65% if you add a picture" (pp. 223-234).

3. **Iterate**. Throughout the semester, keep reminding students of the importance of Bloom's Taxonomy. Have them make Bloom part of their metacognitive processes (see chapter on Metacognition). Since you intend to test the way Hal and Charlie did at this chapter's beginning—i.e., forcing your students to use higher-order skills — it stands to reason that your class

time will provide examples from you and exercises for them that demand application, analysis, evaluation, and creation (more on this topic and alignment in our upcoming chapter on Presenting). Hal and Charlie started every class with a quiz for a lot of reasons, but now they realize an important purpose was to stress that knowledge-building begins with a strong foundation of remembering and understanding. Inculcate the principle of **meaningful learning** that goes beyond roting your assessments and exercises. Bush, Daddysman, and Charnigo (2014) claim, "meaningful learning requires students to use learned information in new ways to solve problems; meaningful learning gives students the tools for understanding new concepts" (1).

One tool for helping students understand what level of Bloom is called for by a test is what Crowe, Dirks, and Wenderoth (2008) call the Bloom Biology Tool. After noting that "each discipline must define the original [Bloom] classifications within the context of their field" (369), they demonstrate how students can be asked to go over their scored tests and label the questions. Why not take this strategy one step further and ask them to label certain questions with the appropriate Bloom level on the test for credit? In short, provide an opportunity for students to create their own formative assessments throughout the course.

4. **Periodically evaluate your own presentation and testing to ensure you have your eyes on the prize — higher-order thinking**. Do the majority of your assessments, your exercises, and your examples demonstrate higher-order thinking? And don't rely on just your judgement. Invite colleagues into your classroom, asking them to be especially conscious of the type of thinking demanded. Have your students write two-minute papers, journal entries, or even answer reflection questions on tests that ask them to delineate for what level of thinking you called. Sure, students can get lucky and use higher-order thinking skills without iteration and some form of evaluation that pinpoints the absence of such training, but remember the principle of intentionality—it's better to do it on purpose. And don't wait until the end of the course when it's too late to evaluate.

*Why not take this strategy one step further and ask them to label certain questions with the appropriate Bloom level on the test for credit?*

## KEY CONCEPTS

- The original Bloom's Taxonomy (1956) provides a framework of educational goals.

- The Revised Bloom's Taxonomy (2001) is a more dynamic taxonomy as emphasized by its use of verbs and gerunds rather than nouns.

- In order to bridge the learning gap, faculty must intentionally teach Bloom's Taxonomy and offer a rationale for its importance to their students.

- Bloom's Staircase provides a hierarchical way to teach Bloom's Taxonomy.

# DISCUSSION QUESTIONS

1. Do you think it matters in either the original or the revised version of Bloom's Taxonomy if the higher-order skills are viewed as a hierarchy?

2. Collaborate with someone from a different discipline than yours. Do you think Bloom's Taxonomy is equally applicable to the two fields, especially if they are far apart (e.g., not as similar as art and literature)?

**BRIDLE: Bloom**

Directions: Evaluate yourself.

Scale: 1=Very Strong, 2=Strong, 3=Moderate, 4=Weak, 5=Very Weak

| SCORE | DESCRIPTOR | COMMENTS |
|---|---|---|
| | SLOs reflect an emphasis on higher-order over lower-order skills | |
| | Assignments (in and out of class) reflect an emphasis on higher-order over lower-order skills | |
| | Assessments (tests, papers) reflect an emphasis on higher-order over lower-order skills | |
| | Class discussions promote the use of higher-order skills | |
| | Rationale is intentionally provided to the students on the importance of Bloom's Taxonomy in deep learning | |

# REFERENCES

Anderson, L., & Krathwohl, D. (Eds.). (2001). *A taxonomy for learning, teaching and assessing: A revision of Bloom's taxonomy of educational objectives* (Complete edition). New York: Longman.

Bloom, B. et al. (1956). *Taxonomy of educational objectives: The classification of educational goals. Handbook 1: Cognitive domain.* New York: Longman.

Bush, H., Daddysman, J., & Charnigo, R. (2014). Improving outcomes with Bloom's taxonomy: From statistics education to research partnerships. *Journal of Biometrics and Biostatistics, 5*(4), 1-3.

Cook, E., Kennedy, E., & McGuire, S. (2013). Effect of teaching metacognitive learning strategies on performance in general chemistry courses. *Journal of Chemical Education, 90*, 961-967.

Crowe, A., Dirks, C., & Wenderoth, M. (2008, Winter). Biology in Bloom: Implementing Bloom's taxonomy to enhance student learning in biology. *CBE—Life Sciences Education, 7*, 368-381.

McGuire, S., & McGuire, S. (2015). *Teach students how to learn.* Sterling, VA: Stylus.

Medina, J. (2008). *Brain rules.* Seattle: Pear Press.

# 6. STRATEGY II: Presenting for Deep Learning

**LEARNING QUIZ** (True or False)

1. The lecture paradigm encourages deep learning.

2. The "Meddler-in-the-Middle" paradigm was created in the late 19th century.

3. Student attention span during a class lecture is estimated at around 30 minutes.

4. Gerald Nosich introduced the term "fundamental and powerful concepts."

5. "Guide on the Side" is the term used for the instructor in the Active Learning paradigm.

## PRESENTATION PARADIGMS

In the 35-plus years that we have been observing classroom teachers at Eastern Kentucky University (EKU), whether they are novice or seasoned instructor, one mode of presentation has dominated. Our discussion with these teachers reveals that they, like the college teachers studied by Halpern and Hakel (2003), "teach the way they were taught" (37)—with the **Lecture**. And if we can believe our counterparts at other schools, the lecture's preeminence is pervasive. In fact, a 1998 survey of one-third of all faculty in this country discovered that 76% identified the lecture as their principal instructional approach (Finkelstein, Seal, and Schuster, 1998). If, however, as we claim in our *Achieving Excellence in Teaching* (2014), "Your primary goal as an excellent teacher is to produce deep learning" (5), the lecture might not be the most effective approach. Let's look at this traditional paradigm as well as several alternatives in order to ascertain which is better for producing deep learning and why.

## The Sage on the Stage

Teaching-learning paradigms, much like art and literature, reflect the culture that produces them, and the lecture method has a longstanding and powerful history. Harkening back to the medieval university with its robed scholars delivering information to silent students, this paradigm depends on an authoritative figure transmitting material to passive recipients. With transmission of information the primary goal, this dynamic served effectively from medieval times through the 19th century's Industrial Revolution, where attentive factory workers could be "trained" in how to operate new-fangled machinery, and even into the 20th century with its classrooms filled with rows of desks fronted by a lectern from which a professor could deliver information as from on high.

During the 20th century the lecture paradigm has come under severe scrutiny. Researchers began to question the effectiveness of the method. Khan (2012), for instance, cites a 1976 study on the ebbs and flows of student attention during a typical lecture session: "the study's authors determined that students needed a three-to five-minute period of settling down, which would be followed by 10 to 18 minutes of optimal focus. Then—no matter how good the teacher or how compelling the subject matter—there would come a lapse. In the vernacular, the students would 'lose it.'" And, worries Khan, since the study was done before today's texting and tweeting culture, we might expect student attention spans are now even shorter and more distracted. In *Brain Rules* (2008) Medina echoes this fear, claiming the average student attention span is somewhere around 12 minutes. Penner (1984) suggests that only 10 minutes of an hour-long lecture gets through before students lose attention. Even worse, McLeish (1968) found early on that a mere hour after a lecture the average student had lost 58% of the information and 90% was gone a month later. Indeed, as Halpern and Hakel (2003) conclude after years of research into learning science, "lecturing is not optimal to foster deep learning" (40).

Perhaps most damning for the lecture as a tool fostering deep learning is its very nature as a transmitter of information. The authoritative voice of the lecturer encourages students to stay at the lower level of Bloom's learning pyramid (see Chapter 5), content to **remember** and **understand**, while as Hieronymi (2012) insists, "Education is not the transmission of information or ideas. Education is the training needed to make use of information and ideas."

## The Guide on the Side

The desire to "make use" of information led to a shift in paradigms toward the end of the 20th century, a shift that moved the balance of authority for teaching and learning toward the students. As Chickering and Gamson (1987) put it, "Students do not learn much just by sitting in classes and

> *Perhaps most damning for the lecture as a tool fostering deep learning is its very nature as a transmitter of information.*

listening to teachers, memorizing prepackaged assignments, and spitting out answers. They must talk about what they are learning, write about it, relate it to experience, and apply it to their daily lives. They must make what they learn part of themselves" (3). Nurtured by individual-empowering movements such as civil rights and feminism, the new paradigm, **Active Learning**, transformed the instructor from an authoritative figure dispensing words of wisdom to a facilitator functioning to help students as they confronted material individually and in groups. While Chickering and Gamson asserted that "Good practice encourages cooperation among students" (3), too often what became known as the **Guide on the Side** surrendered to the temptation simply to put students into groups with little direction/training in group dynamics, monitoring, or assessment. What could have been an effective bridge over the gap between surface and deep learning through teacher-student collaboration frequently fell prey to complaints from students who felt cheated of the expertise of their instructors and held captive in groups wherein they were doing an inordinate amount of the work to cover for poorly prepared classmates.

## Meddler in the Middle

The advances in technology in the early 21st century were accompanied by what Bauman (2004) calls a "liquid modern" social world (22), wherein the key to deep learning has become adaptability, an unlearning of old methodology and a necessity for learning new approaches.

McWilliam (2008) has synthesized cultural and educational research to create the foundation for a new paradigm. Her **Meddler-in-the-Middle** (MIM) model "positions the teacher and student as mutually involved in assembling and disassembling cultural products. . . . Meddling is a repositioning of teacher and student as co-directors of their social world" (88).

As a teaching-learning paradigm, the MIM model calls on the instructor to assume a role quite different from the Sage or even the Guide. For McWilliam, the effective teacher approaches learning in several non-traditional ways:

- "less time giving instructions and more time spent being a usefully ignorant team member in the thick of the action"

- "less time spent being a custodial risk minimizer and more time spent being an experimenter, risk-taker learner"

- "less time spent being a forensic classroom auditor and more time spent being a designer, editor and assembler"

- "less time spent being a counselor and 'best buddy' and more time spent being a collaborative critic and authentic educator." (88)

# Mentor from the Middle

While McWilliam's paradigm provides some insightful suggestions for balancing the relationship between teacher and students to co-facilitate learning that will move students to those higher order levels called for by Bloom, we have never been comfortable with the idea of teacher as meddler. Rather, we like to view the effective instructor as a Mentor who adopts several specific roles in his/her relationship with students:

- As a **facilitator** the mentor is the class's chief organizer, planning schedules, setting goals, assessing to ensure goals are met, and problem solving both theoretical and practical matters;

- As a **coach** the mentor serves as a teacher, motivator, determiner of rules, and damage controller;

- As an **artist** the mentor must be a risk taker, ready to adapt to changing situations, and one who can approach materials from multiple perspectives as well as synthesize disparate elements to create meaningful learning experiences;

- As a **critical reflector** the mentor must constantly examine and evaluate a class session's progress and exercise fair mindedness to achieve that which will produce the best learning experience for all;

- As a **model** the mentor must be aware that students are more apt to develop effective learning skills if they see them embodied in their instructor; and

- As a **scholar** the mentor must establish credibility by staying current in the discipline and in pedagogy through reading, presenting and publishing.

As we point out in *Achieving Excellence in Teaching* (2014), the **Mentor-from-the-Middle** paradigm "takes advantage of technology by having students access the information traditionally disseminated by the lecture and uses class time for deep learning of the material. This paradigm has the advantages of focusing on student learning, being up-to-date with research and technology, sharing the responsibility for learning between mentor and students while retaining mentor authority and placing the mentor literally and figurative in the middle of the learning experience" (63).

*... we like to view the effective instructor as a Mentor who adopts several specific roles in his/her relationship with students...*

## TACTICS FOR USING MENTOR FROM THE MIDDLE IN YOUR CLASS

In addition to our difficulty with the meddler concept in McWilliam's paradigm, we had problems with her minimal illustrations of exactly how the paradigm would work in an actual classroom. In order to bring substance to our new paradigm, therefore, we tried to concentrate on how the mentor could present material in such a way that would foster deep learning. Realizing the importance of structure for each class session and remembering a constant complaint from students in classes we observed that they never knew how one session related to others, we developed an organizing principle we call "Keeping It C.R.I.S.P." (2008):

- **Contextualize**. In each session focus on what Nosich (2009) calls the fundamental and powerful concept(s) for the day. At the beginning of class let students know the major points to be covered.

- **Review**. Point out how the session's fundamental and powerful concept relates to the course's overall focus and how the day's work relates to what has come in previous classes.

- **Iterate**. Repeat the concept throughout the session, trying to use as many different vehicles (speech, PowerPoint, examples, board work) as possible.

- **Summarize**. Pull together the materials from the session, emphasizing the fundamental and powerful concepts. Perhaps even leave a few minutes for students to comment or write a brief paragraph on the concepts covered.

- **Preview**. Suggest some specific things you wish students to look for in the readings for next session. Emphasize the tie to the current session and the course's overall fundamental and powerful concepts.

To aid in CRISPing your class sessions, we developed a six-phase approach that not only assures a balance of mentor-student authority and responsibility, but also enhances the depth of the learning experience.

- **Information Gathering**: using a variety of sources outside the class, the mentor has students do some groundwork in addition to the reading assignment before a given session to prepare for the next class.

- **Crystallizing**: the mentor synthesizes the variety of materials brought to the session by students, careful to point out each offering's relationship to the fundamental and powerful concept emphasized during the session. Perhaps the best way to deliver this synthesis, given what research tells us about attention spans, is to make use of the mini-lecture (approximately ten minutes).

- **Creating the Project**: the mentor decides how to use the synthesized materials to collaborate with students in the creation of a project that will "bring life" to the fundamental and powerful concept at issue. Often this step involves question-answer, discussions, brainstorming, and even such technical approaches as clickers.

- **Completing the Project**: the mentor-student collaboration actually produces something based on the newly-synthesized materials.

- **Skill Making**: the mentor makes students aware of the implications of their work and the attendant transferable skills they've acquired while carrying out the project.

- **Evaluating the Learning Unit**: the mentor has students reflect on their experience verbally, through writing or even concept maps to demonstrate the depth of their learning.

Indeed, presenting has come a long way since those bygone days of the robed scholars. Our Mentor from the Middle provides a way for you to present material in such a way as to promote deep learning, to help your students cross the Learning Gap to the highest levels of Bloom's pyramid.

# KEY CONCEPTS

- Teaching and Learning paradigms are the products of the age that produces them.

- The Lecture paradigm focuses on an authority delivering information to a passive audience.

- The Active Learning paradigm transfers much of the authority and responsibility for learning to the student.

- The Meddler-in-the-Middle paradigm views the teacher and students as co-facilitators of knowledge.

- The Mentor-from-the-Middle paradigm assigns the teacher a variety of roles: facilitator, coach, artist, critical reflector, model, and scholar.

- C.R.I.S.P. is a class organizational model that asks the instructor to **c**ontextualize, **r**eview, **i**terate, **s**ummarize, and **p**review during each class session, focusing on fundamental and powerful concepts (good organization on the instructor's part prepares the student more effectively for deep learning).

- The Mentor-from-the-Middle paradigm establishes a six-phase approach to creating projects promoting deep learning that involves information gathering, crystallizing materials, creating the project, completing the project, skill making, and evaluating the learning unit.

# DISCUSSION QUESTIONS

1. Do you think each class should begin with the professor's placing the day's fundamental and powerful concepts on a whiteboard/blackboard/PowerPoint, or should the professor ask the class at the beginning for what their homework/reading has shown them to be fundamental and powerful concepts? Should the professor vary the approach?

2. Why do you think the lecture method still persists as the major instructional approach (90% by one study) in America's P-20 classrooms?

3. What are some ways that collaboration between teacher and students and among students can best be accomplished?

**BRIDLE: Presenting**

Directions: Evaluate yourself.

Scale: 1=Very Strong, 2=Strong, 3=Moderate, 4=Weak, 5=Very Weak

| SCORE | DESCRIPTOR | COMMENTS |
|---|---|---|
| | Effectively uses the mini-lecture rather than the full-period lecture | |
| | Provides time for students' active learning through group/solitary in-class work | |
| | Provides time for students' active learning through oral/written reflection | |
| | Views self as co-facilitator with the student of deep learning | |
| | Utilizes the C.R.I.S.P. approach to deep learning | |

# REFERENCES

Bauman, Z. (2004). Liquid sociality. In N. Game (Ed). *The future of social theory* (pp. 17-46). London: Continuum.

Bloom, B. et al. (1956). *Taxonomy of educational objectives: The classification of educational goals. Handbook 1: Cognitive domain.* New York: Longman.

Blythe, H. & Sweet, C. (2008). Keeping it C.R.I.S.P. *NEA Higher Education Advocate, 26*(2), 5-8.

Chickering, A. & Gamson, Z. (1987). Seven principles for good practice in undergraduate education. *American Association for Higher Education Bulletin, 39*(7), 3-7.

Finkelstein, M., Seal, R., & Schuster, J. (1998). *The new American generation.* Baltimore: Johns Hopkins University Press.

Halpern, D., & Hakel, M. (2003, July/August). Applying the science of learning to the university and beyond: Teaching for long-term retention and transfer. *Change*, 36-40.

Hieronymi, P. (2012). *Don't confuse technology with college teaching.* Retrieved from http://chronicle.com/2012/08/13/don't-confuse-technology/

Khan, S. (2012). Why long lectures are ineffective. Retrieved from http://ideas.time.com/2012/10/02/why-lectures-are-ineffective/

McLeish. J. (1965). *The lecture method.* Cambridge, England: Cambridge Institute of Education.

McWilliam, Ed. (2008). *The creative workforce: How to launch young people into high-flying futures.* Sidney, Australia: University of New South Wales Press.

Medina, J. (2008). *Brain rules.* Seattle, WA: Pear Press.

Nosich, G. (2008). *Learning to think things through.* Upper Saddle River, NJ: Prentice Hall.

Penner, J. (1984). *Why many college teachers cannot lecture.* Springfield, IL: Thomas.

Sweet, C., Blythe, H., Phillips, B., & Daniel, C. *Achieving excellence in teaching.* Stillwater, OK: New Forums.

# 7. Strategy III: Retrieving for Deep Learning

**LEARNING QUIZ** (True or False)

1. Retrieval is a concept not applicable to quizzing.

2. Multiple sessions, spaced-out practices, varying practices, and expending effort are all good retrieval tactics.

3. Effective feedback must always come from the instructor.

4. Mastery of materials is a more reasonable goal for student learning in a semester-long class than expertise.

5. The so-called testing effect is not scientifically valid.

## BACKGROUND

As mentioned in Chapter 5, with every course Hal and Charlie ever taught, first-year through graduate, they started the class with a quiz. Back then, they had a simpler rationale for the practice:

- Students were more apt to read an assignment on which they knew they were being quizzed.

- Students could pick up a high score on 20% of their final course grade just be reading the material.

- The quiz ensured class started on time, as questions were never repeated.

- The quiz provided a roll call, essential since because of federal aid we had to know who attended each class.

- The quiz provided an excellent launching pad for class discussion, solidifying the old knowledge on which the new was to be built.

- The quiz gave students confidence and interest in the class discussion since they had encountered the material in their reading.

- The quiz offered iteration of key concepts.

Obviously, Hal and Charlie had sufficient reasons for their daily quiz practice, but in retrospect they omitted probably the most important reason, **retrieval**.

Recently, research, especially in cognitive psychology, has recognized the importance of retrieval. Halpern and Hazel (2003) argue that "The single most important variable in promoting long-term retention and transfer is 'practice at retrieval'.... Simply stated information that is frequently retrieved becomes more retrievable. In the jargon of cognitive psychology, the strength of the 'memory trace' for any information that is recalled grows stronger with each retrieval" (38). Brown, Roediger, and McDaniel (2014) define retrieval simply as "recalling facts or concepts or events from memory" (3). In fact, the trio support Hal and Charlie's usage of quizzes: "A single, simple quiz after reading a text or hearing a lecture produces better learning and remembering than rereading" (3). They also stress that "if we stop thinking of testing as a dipstick to measure learning—if we think of it as practicing retrieval of learning from memory rather than 'testing,' we open ourselves to another possibility: *the use of testing as a tool for learning*" (19). Various studies have shown how students tend to forget from 70 to 90% of what they hear in class, but according to Brown et al, "practicing retrieval makes learning stick far better than re-exposure to the original does" (28). Karpicke stresses frequent retrieval, for, "every time a person retrieves knowledge, that knowledge is changed, because retrieving knowledge improves one's ability to retrieve it again in the future. Practicing retrieval does not merely produce rote, transient learning; it produces meaningful, long-term learning" (159).

Frequent retrieval fosters deep learning, but do quizzes actually foster deep learning? Roberts and Roberts (2008) argue against the practice as "quizzes often encourage college students only to learn key words and other concepts at the knowledge level of Benjamin Bloom's taxonomy (Bloom 1956). In short, they encourage surface learning based in episodic memory—short-term memorization for a day or two—rather than deep learning that is transformative of one's perspective and involves long-term comprehension (Tagg 2003)" (127). Let's look at the quiz from the perspective of gain or loss. While admittedly students must place certain facts and concepts in their short-term memory, they still must retrieve them for a quiz. If a quiz is actually a lead-in to deeper learning during the class, the student will then be attaching those new surface details to things already learned—i.e., old knowledge. Think of the quiz, then, as the foundation of deeper learning, or, to use another metaphor, the quiz is a way of priming the learning pump.

> *Recently, research, especially in cognitive psychology, has recognized the importance of retrieval.*

# TACTICS FOR USING RETRIEVAL IN YOUR CLASSES

Retrieval is easier when students focus on the major, over-riding ideas in a course rather than learning every little detail in the course. Nosich (2009) refers to such ideas as fundamental and powerful concepts: "A fundamental and powerful concept is one that can be used to explain or think about a huge body of questions, problems, information, and situations. All fields have f&p concepts, but there are a relatively small number of them in any particular area" (105-6). Brown, Roediger, and McDaniel (2014) echo this notion: "People who learn to *extract key ideas from new material and organize them into a mental model* and connect that model to prior knowledge show an advantage in learning complex mastery" (6).

After rejecting cramming and rereading, Brown et al offer some guidelines for making learning deep through retrieval practice:

- Using **multiple sessions** rather a one-timer (32).

- Having **spaced-out practices** rather than a mass cram session appears to "embed new learning in long-term memory" through the process of consolidation (49).

- **Varying practices** in different times and places "improves your ability to transfer learning from one situation and apply it successfully to another" (51).

- **Interleaving**: alternating among different subjects.

- **Expending effort**. "The more effort you have to expend to retrieve knowledge or skill, the more the practice of retrieval will retrench it" (79). In essence, they offer scientific proof of the Hanks Principle mentioned in Chapter 5 that the "hard" it what makes it "great."

Deep learning, what Brown et al call "Durable, robust learning," occurs when learners accomplish two tasks: 1) they "recode and consolidate new material from short-term into long-term memory" to anchor it, and they "associate the material with a diverse set of cues that will make" later recall easier. Deep learning demands the material has "practical importance" or "keen emotional weight" in one's life and that it "connects" with "other knowledge that you hold in memory" (77)—i.e., all new knowledge must attach to old.

Retrieval can be enhanced by **feedback** on the application of retrieved material. Ambrose et al (2010) emphasize the importance of feedback in deep learning, whether learners study alone, collaborate with others, or take tests (for practice or for real): "Practice must be coupled with feedback that explicitly communicates about some aspect(s) of student performance" (6). For feedback, sole studiers can use flashcards (probably the best learning tool ever), collaborations can employ other members of the group to evaluate responses, and professors can utilize test/quiz follow-up sessions or even **exam-wrappers**. Most exam-wrappers are self-reflections on graded work, asking such questions as:

- What grade did you expect on this work?

- How much effort did you expend studying?

- Which of the previously mentioned learning strategies did you employ?

- Did you use flashcards, electronic or paper(our favorite)?

- What changes do you expect to make in your preparation for the next assignment?

- Do you see a pattern in questions missed — e.g., you were out of class on the day that fundamental and powerful concept was discussed, you always had trouble with that one with your flashcards (our second favorite)?

The best feedback is always timely and positive. Returning a test after you have given the next test in the sequence or having term papers due on the last day of class and never turning them back are both examples of failing to feedback.

Another key to testing retrieval depends on the way a test is used. While some have argued that multiple choice questions can be crafted for deep learning, Stanger-Hall (2012) found that in science classes a mixed exam format would "increase student learning and higher-level thinking in general" (304). Kornell, Hays, and Bjork (2009) discovered that even unsuccessful retrieval on tests enhances future learning, that "taking challenging tests—instead of avoiding errors—may be one key to effective learning" (989); more specifically, "Unsuccessful retrieval might promote deep processing" (996). Finally, administering a test as a learning tool works— i.e., give the test in close temporal proximity to the reading of material, for as Roediger and Karpicke (2006) report positively about so-called "memory tests," "immediate testing after reading a prose passage promoted better long-term retention than repeatedly studying the passage" (253). Why does this method work? Each time the memory is retrieved, it bubbles up with new associations. Frequent testing, often called the **testing effect**, then, is a methodology that should be employed by teacher and learner alike.

Other retrieval tools for enhancing deep learning exist. Ambrose et al (2010) also stress the importance of providing student learners with an **advance organizer**: "students show greater learning gains when they are given an advance organizer, that is, a set of principles or propositions that provide a cognitive structure to guide the incorporation of new information" (53). Previous chapters have underscored the need for a fundamental and powerful concepts approach to presenting as well as the use of the C.R.I.S.P. approach. Another useful tactic is **concept mapping**, which Brown et al (2014) define as "a technique that helps people represent their knowledge visually. . . . Once you have produced your own concept map, the central organizing principles and key features you use should be easier for you to recognize" (59).

Deep learning is not the same as **expertise**, which Ericsson, Krampe, and Tesch-Romer (1993) explain is deliberate practice or "the result of intense practice extended for a minimum of 10 years" (363). Instead, instructors push their students toward something in which the former has already achieved **mastery**, which Brown et al (2014) define as "the attainment of a high degree of competence within a particular area. . . . For students to achieve mastery within a domain, whether narrowly or broadly conceived, they need to develop a set of component skills, practice them to the point where they can be combined fluently and used with a fair degree of automaticity, and know when and where to apply them appropriately" (95).

Another successful retrieval tactic we borrowed called S-E-E-I (see Nosich, pp. 33-37) or the Seeing I technique we now label as **S3P** because we made some refinements in the original. After introducing a new fundamental and powerful concept (FPC), have students take out a piece of paper/laptop and write out four sentences:

- **S**tate the new FPC.

- **P**araphrase the FPC.

- **P**rovide an example of the FPC (that was not used in either the textbook or in class by an instructor or classmate).

- **P**repare a metaphor that embodies the FPC (e.g., "The [FPC] is like . . .).

Ultimately, instructors must use class time (and the first class, which is often wasted, may be the best time) to teach and model the best practices of retrieval. Left alone, students will simply reread the material. As Halpern and Hakel (2003) advise, "if deep understanding of the basic principles is what is wanted, then the teaching and learning process needs to be structured accordingly. This means that instructors and learners ought to have clearly articulated goal statements at the start of instruction that guide instructional design and learning activities" (41).

*Another successful retrieval tactic we borrowed called S-E-E-I, or the Seeing I technique we now label as **S3P** because we made some refinements in the original.*

## KEY CONCEPTS

- Retrieval is recalling facts or concepts or events from memory.

- Frequent retrieval fosters deep learning.

- Best practices in retrieval include multiple sessions, spaced-out sessions, varying sessions in different times and places, interleaving subjects, and expending effort.

- Cramming and rereading are not best practices.

- The testing effect, both by self and others, leads to deep learning.

- Immediate feedback after retrieval efforts improves deep learning.

- The S3P strategy aids deep learning.

## DISCUSSION QUESTIONS/EXERCISES

1. Why do you think that students repeatedly practice such poor retrieval skills as cramming and rereading?

2. What would you consider the most fundamental and powerful concept from your discipline? S3P it.

3. How do you see the relationship between long-term memory and deep learning? Is long-term memory a component of deep learning? From your reading of the book so far, what other elements might also be components of deep learning?

**BRIDLE: Retrieving**

Directions: Evaluate yourself.

Scale: 1=Very Strong, 2=Strong, 3=Moderate, 4=Weak, 5=Very Weak

| SCORE | DESCRIPTOR | COMMENTS |
| --- | --- | --- |
| | Intentionally instructs students as to the best practices in retrieving strategies | |
| | Provides frequent retrieval opportunities inside and outside of class | |
| | Offers immediate feedback (when feasible) after student retrieving efforts | |
| | Offers opportunities for practice testing and reflection | |
| | Offers frequent opportunities for S3P strategies | |

# REFERENCES

Amrose, S., Bridges, M., DiPietro, Lovett, M., & Norman, M. (2010). *How learning works*. San Francisco, Jossey-Bass.

Brown, P., Roediger, H. & McDaniel, M. (2014). *Make it stick: The science of successful learning*. Cambridge, MA: The Belknap Press of Harvard University Press.

Ericsson, K., Krampe, R., & Tesch-Romer, C. (1993). The role of deliberate practice in the acquisition of expert performance. *Psychological Review, 100*(3), 363-406.

Halpern, D., & Hakel, M. (2003, July-August). Applying the science of learning. *Change*, 36-41.

Karpicke, J. (2012). Retrieval-based learning: Active retrieval promotes meaningful learning. *Current Directions in Psychological Science, 21*(3), 157-163.

Kornell, N., Hays, M., & Bjork, R. (2009). Unsuccessful retrieval attempts enhance subsequent Learning. *Journal of Experimental Psychology: Learning, memory, and cognition.* 35(4), 989-998.

Nosich, G. (2009). *Learning to think things through: A guide to critical thinking across the curriculum* (3rd ed.). Upper Saddle River, NJ: Pearson.

Roberts, J. & Roberts, K. (2008). Deep reading, cost/benefit, and the construction of meaning: Enhancing reading comprehension and deep learning in sociology courses. *Teaching Sociology, 36*, 125-140.

Roediger, H. & Karpicke, J. (2006). Test-enhanced learning: Taking memory tests improves long-term retention. *Psychological Science, 17*(3), 249-255.

Stanger-Hall, K. (2012). Multiple-choice exams: An obstacle for higher-level thinking in introductory science classes. *CBE—Life Sciences Education, 11*, 294-306.

# 8. STRATEGY IV: Fostering Metacognition for Deep Learning

**LEARNING QUIZ** (True or False)

1. Metacognition can enhance deep-learning across disciplines.

2. Faculty can teach metacognition strategies to their students.

3. Students should learn approaches for growth mindset before metacognition strategies.

4. Metacognition is best taught at the end of the course.

5. Faculty can incorporate metacognition into any class across the disciplines.

## BACKGROUND

Across the country, institutions of higher education are searching for successful strategies for increasing retention rates among undergraduate students. Thus, many educators have focused not only on strategies for enhancing the student learning experience in the class but outside of it as well. At other institutions, like our own, faculty members are actively examining best practices that enable them to teach for deep learning, the "essence" of which is "understanding—true knowing" (Weimer, 2012). An appropriate consideration, Weimer asks why students "memorize isolated facts" without truly developing an understanding of the course material? We are often confronted with similar questions as we link teaching and learning on our campus.

As a way of understanding metacognition's role in teaching for deep learning, let's begin with a review of our earlier chapters by examining what Weimer calls passive learning and active learning. Passive learning might include, for example, the student simply attending class — that is, showing up and sitting in the back of the room. In passive learning, the student might take notes with no real agenda or planning involved. Furthermore, the student might create index cards or highlight the text. A student might even purchase the book. All of these learning behaviors necessitate *some* level of cognitive engagement from the student but do not always promote deep learning; i.e., the student has not employed strategies that promote long-term learning for understanding or deep learning.

By way of comparison, active learning promotes activities that engage students beyond memorization. Using active learning, students employ collaborative or hands-on techniques that allow them to receive the content while practicing the material. These techniques contribute to deep learning, during which students gain strategies that they can employ in the future and transfer to other learning situations. Often, however, students do not understand the difference between deep learning and surface learning. Let's review the differences between surface learning and deep learning in more detail before examining metacognition.

Oftentimes, students employ surface learning because they do not understand more productive forms of studying, writing, or even researching — that is, they opt for the short-term solution to survive the learning task. Learning is driven, then, more by passing the task than retaining subject knowledge, and in no case is the student's goal to retain knowledge for transfer to another learning task, situation, or assignment. As you might expect, the student-learning cycle repeats in unproductive and, in most cases, unsuccessful ways. However, Table 1, offers a comparison of surface (or what we call passive) learning and deep learning through metacognition.

| Surface (Passive) Learning | Deep Learning through Metacognition |
|---|---|
| Reading and reviewing what is required | Transferring knowledge gained through reading to other academic applications |
| Not reflecting on process or deeper meaning | Annotating readings in the margins or reverse outlining for trends |
| Memorizing facts | Engaging content critically and creatively |
| Writing a paper the night before | Employing a full brainstorming, drafting, revision, feedback, and editing process and reflecting post-process |

**Table 1. Comparison of Surface Learning and Deep Learning through Metacognition**

In summary, "[s]tudents who take a deep approach have the intention of understanding, engaging with, operating in and valuing the subject" (Lublin 3). Deep learning, as we have argued, goes beyond viewing the student as independent recipient of information. The learning process is more involved, sustained, and involves systematic strategies, especially through metacognition.

# TACTICS FOR FOSTERING METACOGNITIVE DEEP LEARNING

We turn, then, to a prominent strategy for enhancing teaching for deep learning: metacognition. While many definitions of metacognition exist, a simplified definition that is easily adapted for a variety of teaching and learning contexts is "thinking about thinking." Some scholars even claim that a field of metacognition exists (Tanner 113). Tanner, in teaching undergraduate biology courses, proposes sample self-questions that "promote student metacognition about learning" (115). Making important distinctions, Tanner separates metacognitive learning strategies by activity, including class session, active-learning task and/or homework, quiz or exam, and overall course (115). What is, perhaps, most interesting is that Tanner also assigns activities to process-based stages that include planning, monitoring, and evaluating. Saunda McGuire (2015), a nationally known metacognition scholar and proponent, builds on these definitions of metacognition by claiming that it is also the ability to "be consciously aware of oneself as a problem solver." In addition, she explains that metacognition involves monitoring, planning, and controlling one's mental processing," "accurately judging one's level of learning," and knowing "about one's knowledge." Importantly, McGuire and McGuire (2015) argue that we can, in fact, teach students to learn better, retain classroom content, and transfer learned material through metacognition. To this end, as McGuire and McGuire contend, "we should be at least as focused on student learning we are on our teaching" (9).

*...we can, in fact, teach students to learn better, retain classroom content, and transfer learned material through metacognition.*

Moving forward, we would like to highlight Tanner's process-based approach and build on these three phases. Simply put, Tanner's processes encourage student learning through **intentional questioning**. For planning, students are taught to question their goals for learning. Monitoring prompts students to question insights they are having related to the class session (or during the learning experience). In evaluating, students are asked to reflect by posing questions such as "What was today's class session about?" (115). Tanner's succinct approach reinforces the point that metacognitive learning is *intentional* learning. It is planned and implemented, and students can then articulate what it is and when it is happening or how well the learning strategy worked.

Building on Tanner's model of intentional questioning, Emily Vinson, an undergraduate research assistant in EKU's Noel Studio for Academic Creativity, the University's primary teaching and learning research program, examined pedagogical practices among trained peer consultants as they provided feedback on communication-design processes among undergraduate students. Based on this research, Vinson (2015) suggests that the metacognition learning process in the Noel Studio, where students can complete an entire learning cycle, with and without faculty, extends far beyond questioning but is equally intentional. What's interesting about Vinson's observations is that metacognition transcends space and discipline (see Figure 1).

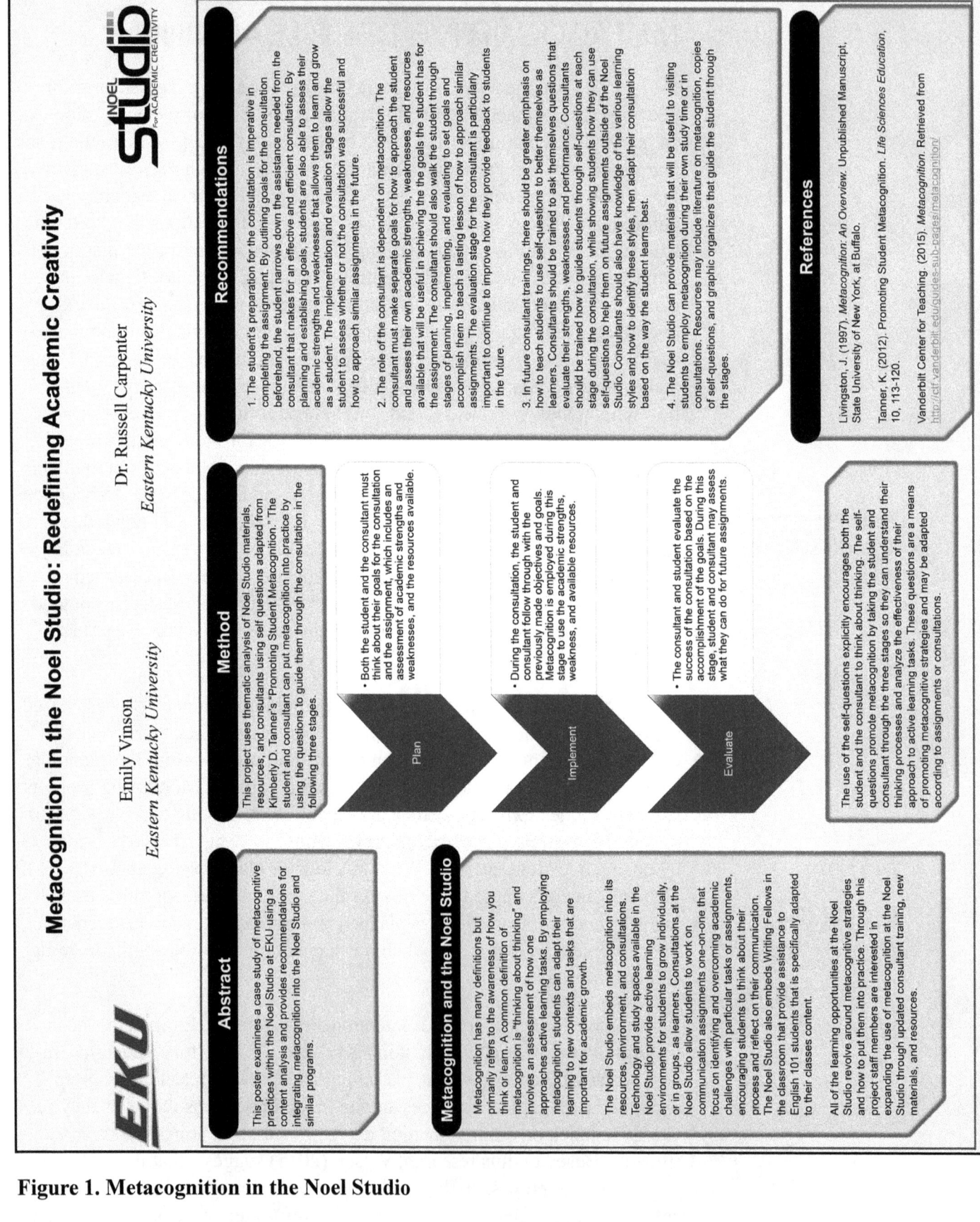

Figure 1. Metacognition in the Noel Studio

# LINKING DEEP LEARNING AND METACOGNITION

The National Research Council (2000) explains that "Metacognition can help students develop personally relevant pedagogical content knowledge, analogous to the pedagogical content knowledge available to effective teachers . . . In short, students need to develop the ability to teach themselves" (50). Additionally, Matthew Kaplan, Naomi Silver, Danielle Lavaque-Manty, and Deborah Meizlish (2013) argue, "One way to engage students is to help them become involved in and responsible for their own learning, making decisions about how they go about learning in addition to deciding what they want to learn and how they want to use that learning" (3). Taken together, these two perspectives link student learning with metacognition in several ways, by promoting:

- Independent learning

- Students as responsible collaborators in the teaching and learning experience

- Ways in which teachers might reveal learning to students

- Ways in which teachers explain and articulate metacognition strategies to students, and

- Strategies for encouraging students to reflect not only on what they learned but *how* they learned it.

*Metacognition is successful only when students are aware of the approach and process, especially as they impact and enhance deep learning.*

Metacognition is successful only when students are aware of the approach and process, especially as they impact and enhance deep learning. In Table 2, we offer more detailed explanations and strategies for how teaching guides students to deep learning through metacognitive approaches. Teachers can focus on metacognitive approaches in their own instruction and in the student learning experience to achieve deep learning.

|  | Metacognition | Deep Learning |
|---|---|---|
| Facilitating independent learning | Students become responsible for their own learning inside and outside the classroom | Students develop understanding for the most effective ways to prepare themselves to learn and articulate how these approaches transfer to other courses |
| Collaborating with students in the teaching and learning experience | Students see themselves as central to the learning process and experience | Students embrace the challenge of complex learning experiences through low- and high-stakes situations; students co-construct knowledge |

| Revealing learning to students | Discuss metacognition; define metacognition in an early class and refer to this discussion throughout the semester; discuss specific metacognition strategies with students | Students learn to control their own learning and understanding how their successes were achieved; they can then identify these concepts as appropriate in the future |
|---|---|---|
| Explaining and articulating metacognition strategies to students | Students learn specific and measurable approaches applicable in any learning situation | Students learn not only content but about their learning habits, both productive and unproductive |
| Encouraging students to reflect not only on what they learned but *how* they learned it | Students see the purpose of the work and learning | Students adopt strategies that work best for them and understand in which learning situations they are best used |

**Table 2. Making Visible Links Between Metacognition and Deep Learning**

The strategies in Table 2 begin the process. However, it is critical that teachers create learning spaces for these experiences to occur through their own teaching (see "Creating Spaces for Deep Learning"). By teaching specifically for metacognition, teachers have a better chance to also *teach for* and *achieve* deep learning. Implicit within this teaching and learning relationship is fostering a learning-centered mindset in students through excellent teaching environments.

# DEEP LEARNING, MINDSET, AND METACOGNITION

Using metacognition to promote deep learning among students requires establishing the students as willing and interested learners in the first place. Dwek (2006) promotes a growth mindset, the "belief that your basic qualities are things you can cultivate through your efforts. Although people may differ in every which way—in their initial talents and aptitudes, interests, or temperaments—everyone can change and grow through application and experience" (7). Teaching for deep learning means that we are also teaching students to change their mindset toward learning and, perhaps most importantly, to the learning process. The approach involves cultivating a willingness to learn not only content but also how that content knowledge was acquired. From the beginning of class, we can employ metacognitive strategies to enhance the learning experience and success rates of students in our classes. To this end, however, we might begin with discussing and promoting the growth mindset in students so that they are prepared to receive these new learning strategies. As such, growth mindset becomes an important *teaching strategy* in the process as well. Figure 2 provides a pattern for thinking about these concepts in the classroom.

**Figure 2. A model for achieving deep learning through metacognition**

In Figure 2, we see the importance of establishing the growth mindset in students so that they are prepared to receive, and understand the significance of, metacognition strategies. Establishing growth mindset in students first before providing them with metacognitive strategies as part of their day-to-date learning experience prepares them to master their own learning process long before the first quiz or exam.

Once you have established the growth mindset, you can establish metacognitive strategies as central to what Brown, Roediger, and McDaniel (2014) call effortful learning (3). A focus on effortful learning suggests to students that learning takes hard work and a willingness to grow. Moreover, students also repeat learning strategies that are successful in different situations, an approach that Medina (2014) claims "fixes memories" (148). Instilling a growth mindset in students ensures that they are willing to take that learning journey with us and, because you've overviewed and provided examples of metacognitive approaches, your teaching is enhanced at the same time. That is, metacognition and deep learning run on complementary paths in that one supports and enables the other, or as Figure 1 shows, metacognition is the path to deep learning, the ultimate teaching goal.

When deep learning is achieved, we can note a change in attitude toward learning and learning processes. If students can articulate what it is that they think, teach it, and then reflect on the process to understand what made it successful, we've taught a full deep-learning cycle through metacognition (Figure 3).

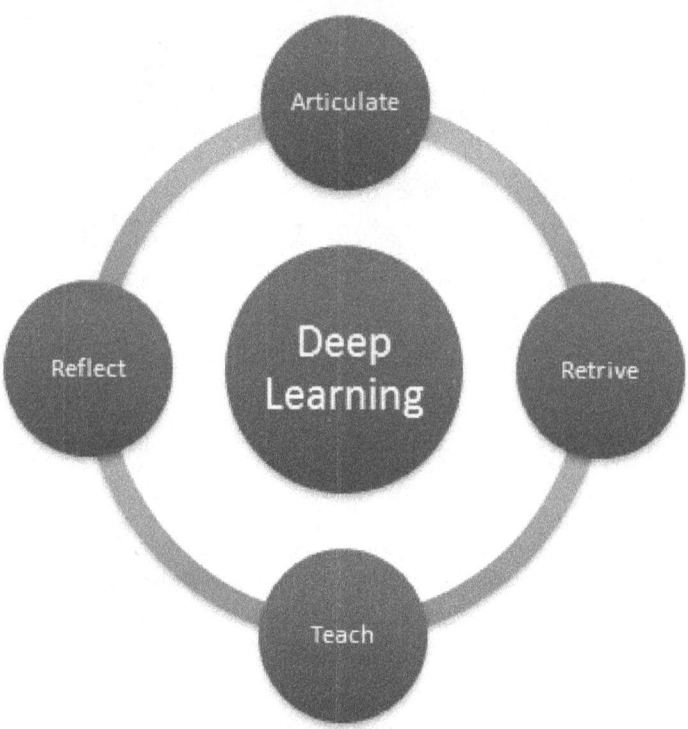

**Figure 3. Teaching Deep Learning through Metacognition Cycle**

In Figure 3, articulating, retrieving, teaching, and reflecting connect to form a process that helps instructors achieve the goal of teaching for deep learning. These four strategies operate best if employed in order, beginning with articulating and moving to retrieving and teaching. Although we do not mean to suggest that the deep-learning process is necessarily rigid, we promote the importance of having students experience each in this order to ensure that learning is taking place. Students can also use the ARTS inventory as an instrument for measuring and assessing their own deep learning throughout the process (see Appendix C). Instructors can administer the ARTS, which is designed to help students assess learning, before and after class sessions or workshops.

Moving forward, teachers can articulate the cycle to students, and each component is critical to teaching for deep learning. Furthermore, each individual learning experience, once mastered, is portable across learning situations and academic disciplines. The process itself, then, encourages a growth mindset that empowers student learners through highly effective teaching. Making these learning experiences apparent in your teaching and creating time for them as part of your teaching process can be critical. To teach for deep learning, you must teach students to become active, critical, and creative (or empowered) learners. If you accomplish this feat in your teaching, students will be willing to apply deep learning approaches from your course to others, and we know that they will take to learning tasks that they like more than those that they do not. Or, put another way, students will naturally gravitate to what they think they're good at over what challenges them. When you teach students to employ deep learning in unappealing learning situations (or those that they do not view favorably), you've taught students to learn deeply through metacognition.

We also encourage you to follow along in EKU's social media conversation about metacognition. The Noel Studio has established a memorable hashtag to archive teaching and learning conversations involving metacognition by using #EKUMeta. We welcome you to join us online!

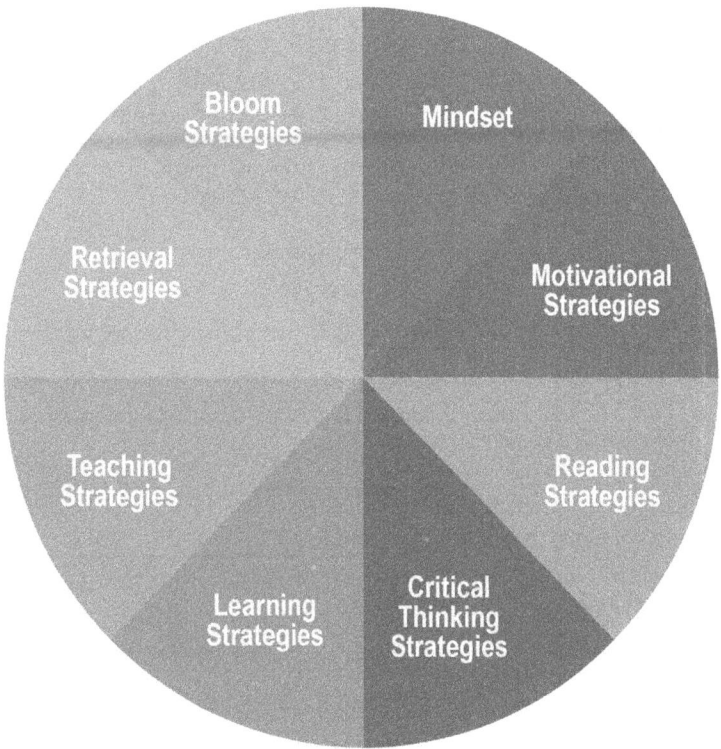

**Figure 4. Metacognition Umbrella**

## KEY CONCEPTS

- Using metacognition to promote deep learning among students requires establishing the students as willing and interested learners in the first place.

- Teaching for deep learning means that we are also teaching students to change their mindset toward learning and to the learning process.

- To teach for deep learning, you must teach students to become active, critical, and creative (or empowered) learners.

# DISCUSSION QUESTIONS

- How might you employ the metacognition cycle to enhance teaching for deep learning in your classroom?

- What challenges might you face when incorporating metacognition into your classroom? How will you confront those challenges in teaching for deep learning and what resources or tools are in place on your campus that you might consult?

- What strategies might you employ in your discipline to incorporate metacognition in teaching for deep learning?

**BRIDLE: Metacognition**

Directions: Evaluate yourself.

Scale: 1=Very Strong, 2=Strong, 3=Moderate, 4=Weak, 5=Very Weak

| SCORE | DESCRIPTOR | COMMENTS |
|---|---|---|
| | Intentionally teaches metacognitive strategies to students early | |
| | Intentionally teaches the mindset concept to students early in course | |
| | Uses the ARTS (or a version of it) to help students monitor their development | |
| | Uses metacognition strategies to foster students' abilities to teach themselves | |

# REFERENCES

Brown, P. C., Roediger III, H., and McDaniel, M. (2014). *Make it stick: The science of successful learning.* Cambridge, MA: Belknap/Harvard.

Dwek, C. (2006). *Mindset: The new psychology of success.* New York: Ballentine.

Kaplan, M., Silver, N., Lavaque-Manty, D., &and Meizlish, D. (2013). *Using reflection and metacognition to improve student learning: Across the disciplines, across the academy.* Sterling, VA: Stylus.

Lublin, J. (n.d.). *Deep, surface and strategic approaches to learning.* Centre for Teaching and Learning: Good Practice in Teaching and Learning. Retrieved from http://www2.warwick.ac.uk/services/ldc/development/pga/introtandl/resources/2a_deep_surfacestrategic_approaches_to_learning.pdf

McGuire, S. (2015, October 30). "Get Students to Focus on Learning Instead of Grades: Metacognition is the Key!" Eastern Kentucky University. Richmond, KY.

McGuire, S. Y., and McGuire, S. (2015). *Teach students how to learn: Strategies you can incorporate into any course to improve student metacognition, study skills, and motivation.* Sterling, VA: Stylus.

Medina, John. (2014). *Brain rules.* Seattle, WA: Pear Press.

National Research Council. (2000). *How people learn: Brain, mind, experiences, and school.* Washington, DC: National Academy Press.

Tanner, Kimberly D. (2012). Promoting student metacognition. *CBE—Life Sciences Education.* 11, 113-120.

Vinson, Emily. (2015, April 17). "Metacognition and the Noel Studio: Redefining Academic Creativity." Undergraduate Poster Showcase. Richmond, KY.

Weimer, Maryellen. (2012). Deep learning vs. surface learning: Getting students to understand the difference. *Faculty Focus.* Retrieved from http://www.facultyfocus.com/articles/teaching-professor-blog/deep-learning-vs-surface-learning-getting-students-to-understand-the-difference/

# 9. STRATEGY V: Developing Critical Thinking for Deep Learning

**LEARNING QUIZ** (True or False)

1. Critical thinking is always negative in nature.

2. Critical thinking considers other points of view.

3. Critical thinking involves thinking about your thinking to improve your thinking while you are thinking.

4. Critical thinking could be defined as evaluating the argument.

5. Critical thinking always considers bias when evaluating evidence.

6. Critical thinking is a synonym for deep learning.

# BACKGROUND

News Alert: "Ninety-seven percent of scientists agree on global warming," reported the nightly news, citing the President at a global conference on environmental issues. Bill, who drives a hybrid car, has an off-grid cabin, and grows most of his own fruits and vegetables, liked what he heard because it aligned with his values and came from seemingly reliable sources (the President of the United States and the nightly news).

However, in a weekly visit with Charlie and Hal, the three of us began to evaluate the assumptions behind the global warming argument. Were they accurate? Did the conclusions make sense? Had we ever known researchers to agree on anything? Did the person who performed the research finding ninety-seven percent agreement have any vested interest in the outcomes? How could we verify that the research was true? What factors might make this a difficult problem? Did we need to consider other points of view?

In our conversation, we drilled down to discuss the methodology of the study cited by the President. Who was surveyed? Was it really all the world's three and a half million scientists? Were they only academic scientists who are actively publishing on the topic of global warming? Were any of them dependent upon federal grants (by a government whose bias is towards global warming) for their livelihood? Was there a random sample to select the researchers surveyed, or were certain criteria used in selection? How was global warming (now usually called climate change) defined for the study?

After the discussion, Bill concluded that before we could possibily evaluate the validity of the President's citation, we would need much more information about the nature of the survey, its methodology, and the scientists who responded to the survey. In addition, we realized that we had to consider where Bill had found this view on global warming, the nightly news. Gerald Nosich (2009) notes that the nightly news has its own bias, toward things that are unusual. Therefore, the stories often present a distorted point of view to make them newsworthy. Things like shark attacks, terrorist bombings, ax murders, even global warming with its doomsday associations of the annihilation of polar bears and the melting of the polar ice cap are all vivid subjects that elicit strong emotions—the so-called "If it bleeds, it leads" approach. The problem is that after a while because of the frequency of these vivid stories, they begin to seem like common occurrences, and our view of the world can become distorted as we're more willing to take things at face value regardless of how shocking. A sweeping claim such as "ninety-seven percent of scientists believe in global warming" is thus likely to be accepted without any sort of critical assessment of its validity. After all, it came from a reliable source on the network news.

Through our evaluation of a global warming argument, we realized the importance of critical thinking in transforming our students from lower-order thinkers to those who use higher-order skills to assure deep learning.

Many definitions can be found in the literature for critical thinking, and all show great variance. Bok (2006) claims critical thinking is "The ability to think critically—to ask pertinent questions, recognize and define problems, identify the arguments on all sides of an issue, search for and use relevant data, and arrive in the end at carefully reasoned judgments" (109). Brookfield emphasizes the need for students to develop a "critically alert cast of mind—one that is skeptical of claims to final truths or ultimate solutions to problems, is open to alternatives, and acknowledges the contextuality of knowledge" (pp. 21-22). Ennis (1962) asserts, "Critical Thinking is reasonable, reflective thinking that is focused on deciding what to believe or do." Lipman (1995) believes that, "Critical Thinking is skillful, responsible thinking that is conducive to good judgment because it is sensitive to context, relies on criteria, and is self-correcting." Paul's (2007) definition is, "Critical Thinking is thinking about your thinking, while you're thinking, in order to make your thinking better." Nosich (2009) suggests that critical thinking is reflective, involves standards, is authentic, and involves being reasonable.

While standards of critical thinking are numerous and varied, we believe they can be reduced (remember Nosich's "fundamental and powerful concepts"). Inspired by reading Elder and Paul's comprehensive *Analytic Thinking* (2007) and *Guide to Critical Thinking* (2009), we distilled their nine Intellectual Standards, eight Elements of Thoughts, and eight Intellectual Traits into six standards of deep thinking—the **PASSOR** Process: Perspective, Accuracy, Sufficiency, Specificity, Objectivity, and Relevancy. Rather than requiring student to remember twenty-five items, we have not only reduced the number of traits, but also provided a simple mnemonic device for recalling them—PASSOR, as in Pass or Fail.

After reading the voluminous and often complex research on critical thinking, we also developed a simplified and synthesized definition of critical thinking: **evaluating the argument.** And since as we learned in our rhetoric classes everything is argument, PASSOR provides a prism for analysis (remember Bloom) of most any subject. To apply critical thinking to deep learning, look through the lens of each of the six standards of thought. To think deeply about any issue, ask questions about:

- **Perspective**. Have counter claims been collected and analyzed? Prepare to argue the issue from both sides. Make a list of the pros and cons.

- **Accuracy**. How can these facts be checked? Triangulation is one means of evaluating facts. Triangulation involves finding three different sources of information to check the validity of a stated opinion.

- **Sufficiency**. Are more details warranted? What are some of the complexities of this problem? Is there a sufficient amount of information and analysis to make a good decision? With the results of the focus group, create questions to survey a random selection of stakeholders.

- **Specificity**. Have you examined the four Ws of Who, What, When, and Where? Who is making the argument, and what is that person's reputation? What does the argument actually claim? Is the supporting evidence recent or has it been superseded? What is the true source of the evidence—a study, an opinion?

- **Objectivity**. Have personal biases been taken into account? Have other points of view been evaluated? Are there other perspectives that have been overlooked? On a piece of paper state your opinion and then look for another perspective that is radically different. Compare and contrast two opinions and identify biases.

- **Relevance**. Does the evidence presented align with the argument? Write the evidence on one side of the paper and the argument on the other. Draw a line through the evidence that is not relevant to the argument.

*PASSOR provides a prism for analysis (remember Bloom) of most any subject.*

Arum and Roksa (2011) in their book *Academically Adrift: Limited Learning on College Campuses* assert that a shift away from academic rigor has occurred, resulting in graduates who cannot think critically, write thoughtfully, or solve complex problems. Colleges have fallen victim to the demand for increasing retention and graduation rates, which has forced professors to dumb down the curriculum, assign less reading, and less writing. Students are not asked nor are they taught to think deeply. A problem arises when a student customer model, which offers lots of extracurricular activities and little academic rigor, drives colleges. This process has resulted in one third of students without any courses that require forty pages of reading a week and one half who do not have to write a twenty-page paper. The sad result is that colleges have focused their attention on enrolling and retaining students rather than educating them to think deeply.

## TACTICS FOR IMPROVING CRITICAL THINKING AND DEEP LEARNING IN THE CLASSROOM

One way of helping students to think critically and learn deeply is to involve them in discussions about current topics in the news. That students learn how to **evaluate the argument** like Charlie, Hal, and Bill did in the discussion about global warming is crucial. Let's go back to that discussion and apply the **PASSOR** Process of critical thinking.

Remember the news alert: "Ninety-seven percent of scientists agree on global warming." Whether you choose this topic or another for an assignment, have them progress through the PASSOR Process.

First, ask questions about **Perspective**. Have counter claims been collected and analyzed? Prepare to argue the issue from both sides. Make a list of the pros and cons. Remember that no pancake is so thin that it does not have two sides. This situation holds true with any issue. Collect information on global warming so that you can argue both sides. Bill, for instance, once had a professor who would pick an issue and argue for it on Tuesday and against it on Thursday. This professor always brought research papers and opinion papers into class to support his arguments. This approach gave perspective on a wide range of current issues in educational psychology and forced students to think critically as they confronted the arguments presented. When Hal and Charlie taught argument in first-year English, they allowed their students to argue for anything they wanted, but in their next paper, the students were required to create the counter argument.

Second, ask questions about **Accuracy**. How can these facts be checked? Dig deeper into the argument by reading the research articles that inspired the news report and the President's citing. Can you locate other

*The sad result is that colleges have focused their attention on enrolling and retaining students rather than educating them to think deeply.*

sources that confirm the original report's accuracy? Remember *All the President's Men* when Woodward and Bernstein could not go to print without two confirming sources? Think of yourself as a fact-checker website deciding whether or not to give the argument a few Pinocchios for lying. Consider what accuracy means in the sciences? Can these findings be replicated by the described methodology and thus confirmed? You don't have to go as far as scientific protocols, but you can't necessarily consider anything "true" just because you read it (on the Internet) or heard it.

Third, ask questions about **Sufficiency**. Are more details warranted? What are some of the complexities of this issue? Is there a sufficient amount of information and analysis to make a good decision? Start with a review of the relevant literature on global warming and then summarize the findings. Ask questions and state the problem in writing. Make sure the right questions are being asked by having a discussion with a focus group on the topic. With the results of the focus group, create questions to survey a random selection of stakeholders.

Fourth, ask questions about **Specificity**. Does the evidence supply a who, what, when, and where? If it's a scientific study, what is the n, how was it arrived at, and is it a large enough number? Does a sample really represent the whole? Evaluate the **who**. Some sources are better than others. For example, who has a better grasp on global warming, that professor teaching environmental sciences or the next student you stop in the quad? What is the who's reputation (does, for instance, the scientist have a history of hysterical pronouncement such as by 2015 the polar cap will have melted)? Is the **what** clearly stated? Why, for example, did global warming suddenly metamorphosize into climate change, a highly ambiguous term? **When** did the evidence appear? Currency matters. More recent sources often cite previous sources. **Where** did the study/research take place, and where was it published? A world of difference exists between JAMA (the official publication of the American Medical Association) and an Internet post by an anonymous blogger.

Fifth, ask questions about **Objectivity**. Have personal bias been taken into account in creating the survey or selecting those surveyed? If it's a survey, do the questions themselves have an explicit or implicit bias? Have other points of view been evaluated? Are there other perspectives that have been overlooked? What about possible biases by those advancing the argument? Can you find other materials that define the arguer's bias?

Sixth, ask questions about **Relevance**. Does the evidence presented align with the argument? The argument claims scientists agree on global warming. The evidence might include that scientists rarely agree on anything as polarizing as global warming. The evidence of global warming should be from several sources and from those scientists qualified to speak on the topic (is a cognitive psychologist, for instance, knowledgeable on this topic?). Now compare the evidence to the argument's claim.

# A FINAL WORD

When using PASSOR, don't worry with which standard you start. The most important thing is to work through all six steps. Sitting on our office desk is an excellent visual aid, a three-dimensional object we call the Critical Thinking Cube. All six sides are approximately 3x3 inch plexi-glass with each pane labelled with one of the six PASSOR standards. Inside the cube sits a rubber model of the brain labelled "Argument." The object of the Cube is to view the argument from six different angles—i.e., evaluating the argument.

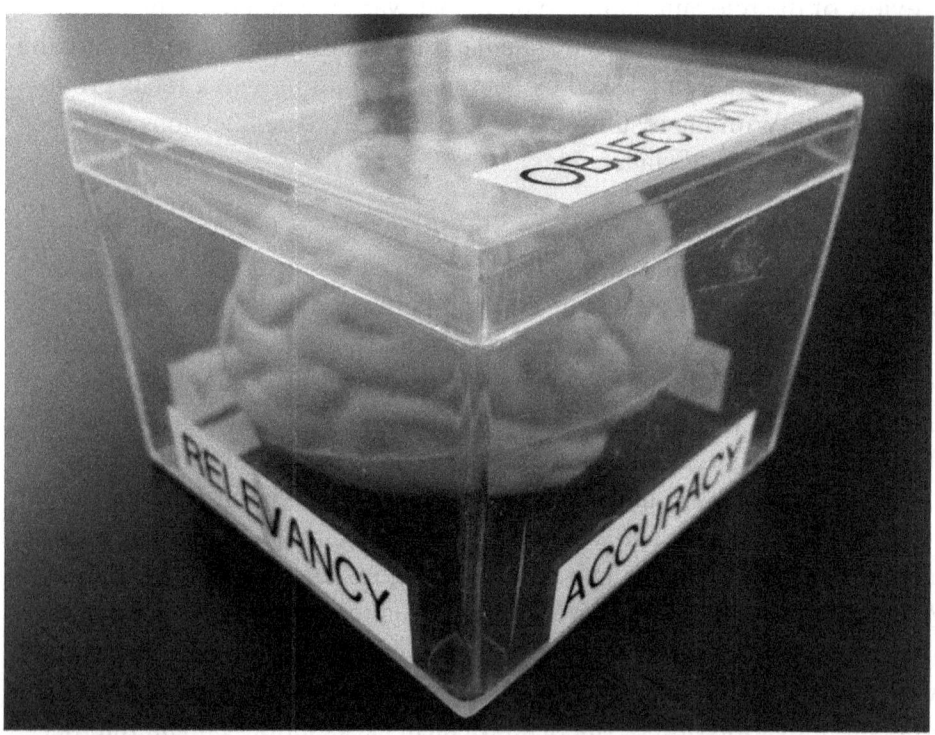

**Figure 1 Low-Resolution Prototype of PASSOR, the Critical Thinking Cube**

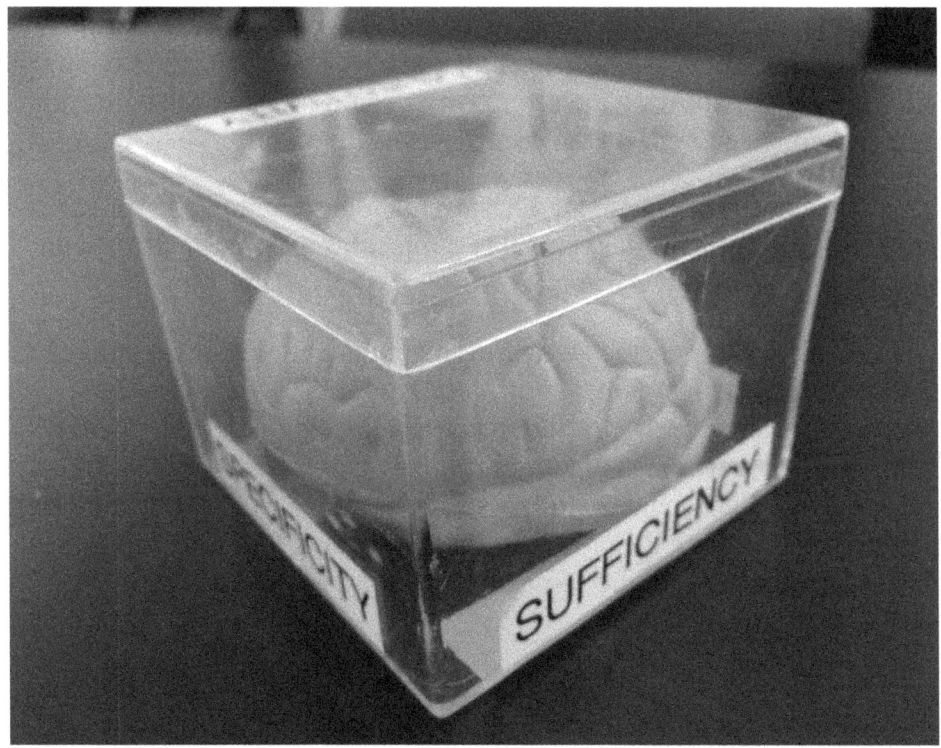

**Figure 2 Low-Resolution Prototype of PASSOR, the Creative Thinking Cube**

## Key Concepts

- Critical thinking can be thought of as **evaluating the argument**.

- Most argumentative claims need to be evaluated through critical thinking.

- The **super six standards** of critical thinking — the PASSOR Process — are Perspective, Accuracy, Sufficiency, Specificity, Objectivity, and Relevancy.

- Through the proper use of critical thinking, students can close the gap between lower-order and higher-order skills, and achieve deep learning.

## DISCUSSION QUESTIONS/EXERCISES

1. Arum and Roksa argue that the majority of America's college students do not develop into critical thinkers. The two researchers have collected a great deal of research to support their premise. Apply the super six standards to their argument to see if you think it is made effectively.

2. Select a controversial question in our society, break the class into six groups, and assign each group one of the PASSOR traits to apply. Then redivide by splitting the groups in two and having each construct a pro or a con argument on the controversial question.

3. Select a controversial decision made by a famous historical figure (e.g., Muhmmad Ali's refusal to subject himself to the draft) and evaluate that decision by using PASSOR.

4. Assign a twenty-page research paper that investigates the pros and cons of any issues. For example, ask students to locate ten references from recent articles by people who believe humans are the major cause of global warming and another ten articles from people who deny global warming. Then have students evaluate the argument by looking critically and thinking deeply about the issue using PASSOR. If you try this assignment early in the semester, you will have adequate time for feedback.

5. The previous assignment sets up the basis for a simplified in-class debate about global warming or any subject.

## BRIDLE: Critical Thinking

Directions: Evaluate yourself.

Scale: 1=Very Strong, 2=Strong, 3=Moderate, 4=Weak, 5=Very Weak

| SCORE | DESCRIPTOR | COMMENTS |
|---|---|---|
| | Utilizes effective critical thinking practices such as the 20+-page paper, debates, and 40 pages of reading/week | |
| | Teaches evaluating the argument through **PASSOR**—**P**erspective | |
| | Teaches evaluating the argument through **PASSOR**--**A**ccuracy | |
| | Teaches evaluating the argument through **PASSOR**--**S**ufficiency | |
| | Teaches evaluating the argument through **PASSOR**--**S**pecificity | |
| | Teaches evaluating the argument through **PASSOR**--**O**bjectivity | |
| | Teaches evaluating the argument through **PASSOR**--**R**elevance | |

# REFERENCES

Arum, R., and Roksa, J. (2011). *Academically adrift: Limited learning on college campuses.* Chicago: University of Chicago Press.

Bok, D. (2006). *Our underachieving colleges.* Princeton, NJ: Princeton University Press.

Brookfield, S. (1990). *The skillful teacher.* San Francisco: Jossey-Bass.

Elder, L., and Paul, R. (2007). *Analytic thinking.* Dillon Beach, CA.: Foundation for Critical Thinking Press.

Elder, L., and Paul, R. (2009). *Guide to critical thinking.* Dillon Beach, CA: Foundation for Critical Thinking.

Ennis, R. (1962). A concept of critical thinking. *Harvard Educational Review, 32,* 81-111.

Lipman, M. (1995). *Thinking in Education.* Cambridge: Cambridge University Press.

Nosich, Gerald. (2009). (3$^{rd}$ ed.) *Learning to think things through: A guide to critical thinking across the curriculum.* Columbus, OH: Pearson, Prentice Hall.

# 10. STRATEGY VI: Employing Deep Reading for Deep Learning

**LEARNING QUIZ** (True or False)

1. The 21st-century digital lifestyle aids the development of deep reading.

2. The K-12 emphasis on comprehension and retention is compatible with deep reading.

3. Deep reading is to surface reading as deep learning is to surface learning.

4. Deep readers become so engrossed in the text that they don't connect it to the real world or their own knowledge.

5. Instructors can provide effective tactics for teaching deep reading.

## BACKGROUND

In terms of the march of time, reading is in its infancy—a mere 5500 years old, according to Wolf and Barzalli (2009) — and back when early human beings roamed 13 miles a day, reading the terrain, not reading books, was the essential survival skill. Ironically, as we enter the digital age, traditional reading seems to be going the way of the dinosaur. Digital media appear to be transforming the way we read. One unintended consequence of the Internet, contends the Envision Blog (2014), "is that our brains have adjusted to this bombardment of information by learning to skim, jump and click from item to item in order to quickly identify what interests us and discard everything else." Wolf and Barzillai (2009) believe, "From a cognitive neuroscience perspective, the digital culture's reinforcement of rapid attentional shifts and multiple sources of distraction can short-circuit the development of the slower, more cognitively demanding comprehension processes that go into the formation of deep reading and deep thinking" (35). Hence, as we mentioned in Chapter 3, Carr refers to the Internet generation as "pancake people."

In addition, as we also delineated in Chapter 3, the K-12 education process promotes surface reading. Roberts and Roberts (2008) explain that "Although children learn the mechanics of reading in elementary grades . .

. The emphasis on 'reading to learn,' that is, reading with a focus on *comprehension and retention* begins in earnest in upper-elementary and middle school. . . . Part of the problem is that reading-to-learn in high school is often reading for factual information to regurgitate (surface learning) rather than reading to make meaning and construct a strong argument (deep learning)" (125).

Roberts and Roberts (2008) bring up another reading problem: college students "do not always complete reading assignments" (126). In a survey of introductory sociology courses, Howard (2004) reported that a mere 40% of students "always or usually" read the assigned text.

And don't forget that college instructors must deal (again, as we noted in Chapter 3) with students who read at a sixth grade, eighth-month reading level. If students have yet to master appropriate grade-level reading, how can even the most concerned college instructor teach deep reading tactics? Our position is that college instructors should not teach remedial reading skills, especially since the overwhelming majority of them have not been trained in this specialized area, but that they should teach the more advanced strategies of deep reading.

## DEFINITION

As with the distinction between surface learning and deep learning, many reading specialists use the dichotomy of surface reading and deep reading. Hermida (2009), for instance, claims, "a deep approach to reading is an approach where the reader uses higher-order cognitive skills such as the ability to analyse, synthesize, solve problems, and thinks meta-cognitively in order to negotiate meanings with the author and to construct new meaning from the text" (27). Wolf and Barzillai (2009) elaborate: "By deep reading, we mean the array of sophisticated processes that propel comprehension and that include inferential and deductive reasoning, analogical skills, critical analysis, reflection, and insight" (32). Roberts and Roberts (2008) explain that deep reading is "reading for long-term retention of the material and for comprehension at a level that can be perspective-transforming—involves constructing meaning as one reads" (125). Deep readers are like Walt Whitman's spider, sending out filament after filament so as to connect what is already known with what is read—i.e., the new knowledge is connected to the old. In our *Introduction to Applied Creative Thinking* (2012) we identified **pattern recognition**, or "the ability to discern the figure in the carpet by weaving together separate strands into a coherent whole" (64), as a component of creative thinking, but pattern recognition is also a trait of the deep reader. In fact, in pointing out the importance of pattern recognition in two related fields, we have just spotted a figure in the carpet of cognitive processes. Roberts and Roberts (2008) claim, "A good reader forms visual images to represent the content being read, connects to emotions, recalls settings and events that are similar to those presented

*If students have yet to master appropriate grade-level reading, how can even the most concerned college instructor teach deep reading tactics?*

in the reading, predicts what will happen next, asks questions, and thinks about the use of language. One of the most important steps, however, is to connect the manuscript we are reading with what we already know and to attach the facts, ideas, concepts, or perspectives to that known material" (126).

To simplify and synthesize, deep readers are active readers, while surface readers play a passive role in the reading process. Your role is to help transform students into active deep readers, which is essential for deep learning. But what steps can you take to promote that transformation?

*To simplify and synthesize, deep readers are active readers, while surface readers play a passive role in the reading process.*

## TACTICS FOR TEACHING DEEP READING

One, the concepts you learned about in Chapter Eight on critical thinking work just as well with deep reading. In essence, by instructing your students in PASSOR, you are betting a perfecta. The students have to learn PASSOR only once, then apply it to deep reading. The key with deep reading, as with critical thinking, is first ascertaining the author's main point. Hermida (2009) makes this tactic obvious in noting, "General categories of analysis to interact with academic texts include the following: (i) reading purpose, (ii) context, (iii) author's thesis, (iv) deconstruction of assumptions, (v) evaluating of author's arguments; and (vi) consequences of author's arguments." A sound academic text will evolve from a solid thesis, and deep reading is possible only after students identify and understand the main point.

Two, help students determine the reading speed needed to grasp an assignment. Some passages can be skimmed—such as asides and repetitious examples—but other sections must be negotiated. Sternberg (1987) argues the problem is that poor readers "do not discriminate in their reading time as a function of reading purpose" (186). Some professors make reading guides or even set up a scale from 1=slow reading required → 5=can be read quickly. The best way to establish the scale is to have previous classes help you make it up by being reflective about their reading times.

Three, as Nosich (2008) suggests, and we have mentioned throughout this book, help your students by establishing early in the course your discipline's central ways of looking at life — i.e., "The Logic of the Field or Discipline" (97) — as well as its most fundamental and powerful concepts. Years of frustration can be reduced to positive feelings when students know what to look for. Truthfully, most disciplines have a course that makes these introductions, but, just as truthfully, not every student takes courses in the order in which they are advised. Use some articles in the field to demonstrate to students what approaches authors take, what assumptions they make, and how each author tries to offer something new. Make them aware that evidence is a tricky thing; while currency carries the day in the sciences, very often the preponderance of evidence sways those in the humanities.

In fact, Hal and Charlie once had an article rejected by a top-flight journal in Victorian Literature because it was "too innovative."

Four, the Envision Blog (2014) emphasizes the importance of something seemingly simple and retro: have your students read their assignments from a paper text, not from a computer monitor. As Marshall McLuhan taught us back in the 60s, the medium is often the message, and what the computer screen says to the student is, "Read me quickly, don't be bombarded with info, skimming beats scrutiny, and click at least every 12 seconds." Paper promotes sustained focus and linear thinking, not scrolling and a distracted eye. Why do you think we didn't make this book available on Kindle? To help students with this digital age disorder, Wolf and Barzillai (2009) recommend computer programs, such as the Center for Applied Special Technology's (CAST) "thinking reader" that "embed[s] within the text different levels of strategic supports that students may call on as needed, such as models that guide them in summarizing what they read." Another CAST program asks readers questions as they are reading, cluing them to highlight certain words and suggesting they apply specific reading strategies—visualize, summarize, predict, and question. How diabolic—using technology to fight technology!

Five, Roberts and Roberts (2008) offer eight strategies, including connecting to the text, summarizing the readings, visualizing key ideas, creating a reading response journal, studying as a group, creating a song or rap, using concept mapping, and a Conversational Roundtable graphic. Parrott and Cherry (2011) suggest creating small groups within your class that meet regularly, complete a set of readings, and provide reading preparation sheets, claiming the "reading group process improves upon Roberts and Roberts's (2008) deep reading strategies in that students engage with readings not only on their own but also in small groups" (364).

# KEY CONCEPTS

- The digital age provides impediments to deep reading, but they can be overcome by effective instructors.

- K-12 education is not necessarily conducive to deep reading.

- Deep reading demands higher-order Bloom skills and metacognition in order to construct meaning as one reads and for long-term retention.

- Deep readers attach the new knowledge they find while perusing manuscripts to what they already know.

- Not every passage must be deeply read, but it takes experience and guidance to know when to skim and when to read deeply.

- Various tactics can transform surface readers into deep readers.

## DISCUSSION QUESTIONS

1. Identify other sources in society that you think contribute to surface reading. How? Have textbooks been "dumbed down" too far? Do newspapers' adopting the *USA Today* approach of trying to tell a story in seven paragraphs or less promote a surface approach? What about our own "simplify and synthesize" approach? The rise of graphic novels?

2. Throughout this book we have been critical of technology's role in negatively impacting the deep learner's mind. Construct a pro-technology argument.

3. Reading is difficult; deep reading is doubly difficult. Do you think that today's culture with the rise of safe zones in colleges, helicopter parents taking over their children's decision-making processes, and even participation trophies (vs. championship) has made the difficult harder to deal with?

4. During the past 50 years, schools have not placed an emphasis on teaching grammar and vocabulary. Students cannot name the various parts of speech and diagram sentences as their grandparents could. In short, does this development present another detriment to deep reading?

**BRIDLE: Deep Reading for Deep Learning**

Directions: Evaluate yourself.

Scale: 1=Very Strong, 2=Strong, 3=Moderate, 4=Weak, 5=Very Weak

| SCORE | DESCRIPTOR | COMMENTS |
|---|---|---|
|  | Provides students practice in applying PASSOR to their reading |  |
|  | Teaches several tactics of deep reading. |  |
|  | Helps students recognize the required reading speed for various assignments |  |
|  | Acquaints students with a given discipline's way of looking at life and that discipline's fundamental and powerful concepts |  |
|  | Makes use of paper texts |  |

# REFERENCES

Carpenter, R., Sweet, C., & Blythe, H. (2012). *Introduction to applied creative thinking.* Stillwater, OK: New Forums.

Carr, N. (2009). *The shallows: What the internet is doing to our brain.* New York: W. W. Norton & Company.

Hermida, J. (2009). The importance of teaching academic reading skills in first-year university courses. *Proceedings of the Association of Atlantic Universities Teaching Showcase, 13,* pp. 26-36. Acadia University. Wolfville, Nova Scotia, Canada.

Howard, J. (2004). Just-In-Time teaching in sociology or how I convinced my students to actually read the assignment. *Teaching Sociology, 34*(4), 385-390.

Envision Experience. (2014, May 27). *When deep reading matters: 7 reasons to choose paper over electronic media.* Retrieved from http://www.envisionexperience.com/plan-your-future/blog-articles/when-deep-reading-matters

Nosich, J. (2009). *Learning to think things through* (3$^{rd}$ ed.). Upper Saddle River, NJ: Pearson.

Robert, J., & Roberts, K. (2008). Deep reading, Cost/Benefit, and the construction of meaning: Enhancing reading comprehension and deep learning in sociology courses. *Teaching Sociology, 34*(2), 125-140.

Sternberg, R. (1987). Teaching intelligence: The application of cognitive psychology in the improvement of intellectual skills. In J. Baron and R. Sternberg (Eds.), *Teaching Thinking Skills: Theory and Practice.* New York: Freeman.

Wolf, M., & Barzillai, M. (2009). The importance of deep reading. *Educational Leadership, 66*(6), 32-37.

# 11. STRATEGY VII: Creating Spaces for Deep Learning

**LEARNING QUIZ** (True or False)

1. Learning space is critical to deep learning.

2. Learning space can enhance or inhibit deep learning.

3. You can adapt a learning space for deep learning.

4. All learning spaces foster deep learning.

5. Collaborative spaces can enhance deep learning.

## BACKGROUND

Institutions across the country and internationally have invested millions in enhancements to learning spaces of a variety of shapes and sizes. Universities even enlist the support of high-priced design and construction firms to research and develop the best learning spaces possible. Obviously, universities have begun to focus attention and funding on learning spaces, understanding that not all spaces are created equal. This chapter examines strategies for creating spaces that encourage deep learning.

Diana G. Oblinger's (2006) *Learning Spaces* initiated much of the recent conversation on learning space design. The premise of Oblinger's collection is that spaces have a significant impact on learning. More recently, collections such as Carpenter's (2013) *Cases on Higher Education Spaces* have examined the complexities of learning space design, considering collaborations and innovations that will guide these decisions on university campuses in the future. Since then, even more attention in higher education has focused on what institutions can do to design highly effective spaces for teaching and learning. The Noel Studio for Academic Creativity at Eastern Kentucky University, commonly highlighted in national publications and on blogs for its innovative design, is one example of an effective space that enhances teaching and learning. This space is home to a variety of programming at the center of the University, including those that support communication design. To this end, research suggests (see Carpenter,

2014; Carpenter & Apostel, 2012; Carpenter, Valley, Napier, & Apostel, 2012; Carpenter, Selfe, Apostel, & Apostel, 2015; McWilliam, Sweet, & Blythe, 2012) that student communication and learning are enhanced through thoughtful design of learning spaces. In addition, space can enhance creativity (Boys, 2011; Sweet, Carpenter, Blythe, & Apostel, 2013) through flexible designs and the creation of teaching and learning-focused galleries where activities and process-oriented artifacts are on display. Furthermore, ideal learning spaces yield effective cross-campus partnerships that involve sustained collaboration (Gardner, Napier, & Carpenter, 2013; Fairchild & Carpenter, 2015). Thus far, however, the role of space on teaching for deep learning has gone unexamined.

## TACTICS FOR DESIGNING SPACE FOR DEEP LEARNING

While we have covered deep learning in great detail in earlier chapters, we must also consider the ways in which our teaching and learning spaces enhance or inhibit deep learning. In the pages that follow, we outline learning space designs that not only enhance teaching but also foster teaching for deep learning.

What should instructors consider when setting up learning spaces to foster deep learning? Foremost, consider what you plan for students to accomplish through your teaching. If your teaching goal is for students to transfer learning to other situations and assignments, learning spaces should make the process visible to other students. Setting up seating in a circle or in small-group clusters can allow students to experience learning in ways that rows, for example, do now. Circles facilitate conversation and equitable participation. Clusters, however, facilitate activities that reinforce learning concepts.

When setting up a space to foster deep learning, we recommend arrival to the classroom at least fifteen minutes in advance to ensure that the furniture and other resources like dry-erase boards are optimized to support your teaching activity and student learning goals for the day. Table 1 outlines several sample classroom furniture configurations based on the design of the Noel Studio that enhance deep learning.

*What should instructors consider when setting up learning spaces to foster deep learning?*

| Space Design | Rationale for Deep Learning |
| --- | --- |
| Circular seating design | Promotes student class participation through large-group discussion |
| Cluster seating (groups of three-five) | Promotes interaction through problem-based activities |
| Visual spaces | Encourage students to make learning visible while sharing with others |

**Table 1. Configurations that Enhance Deep Learning**

Instructors do not often consider the importance of simple spatial decisions in the teaching that make major differences not only in the way that students learn but how they perceive learning. Intentional decisions in space design (Table 1) can guide students physically and cognitively through the learning experience.

What does the traditional classroom arrangement of rows and columns of chairs say about teaching and learning? Most likely, you'd think that the class is going to be lecture-based and that you'll be a passive learner. Your seating arrangement reveals to students your intentions for learning or how you envision learning will unfold. A thoughtful space design reinforces teaching that allows students to learn deeply. Similarly, optimal learning spaces suggest to students that the institution values their academic work. Through your emphasis on space design that enhances deep learning and contributes to effective teaching, students become engaged participants. Table 2 offers strategies for you to use to design learning spaces to facilitate deep learning.

*Similarly, optimal learning spaces suggest to students that the institution values their academic work*

| Learning Space Design | Deep Learning |
|---|---|
| Spaces are designed with multiple possible learning configurations | Students develop understanding for the most effective ways to prepare themselves to learn |
| Spaces are designed with furniture on wheels to allow for flexibility in learning experiences | Students embrace the challenge of complex learning experiences through low- and high-stakes situations; students co-construct knowledge |
| Spaces allow for learning and reflection, collaboration and individual work | Students learn to control their own learning and understanding of how their successes were achieved; they can then identify these concepts as appropriate in the future |
| Spaces are designed as learning galleries to allow others to view processes and techniques | Students learn not only content but about their learning habits, both productive and unproductive |
| Spaces are designed as convergent or divergent | Students adopt strategies that work best for them and understand in which learning situations they are best used |
| Spaces are designed as flexible (including rolling chairs and tables) to facilitate collaboration and movement in the learning process. | Motion reinforces deep-learning activity |

**Table 2. Designing Spaces for Deep Learning**

Space can enhance teaching for deep learning. Design should be intentional and reflective of the teaching and learning situations. Classroom seating configurations can change class to class or activity to activity. We encourage you to experiment with your own classroom setups and to adapt space-design strategies that work for your classroom. We suggest that you also consider:

- Observing students learning in different classroom configurations

- Adapting classroom configurations to fit your teaching goals

- Asking students for feedback on ways in which your teaching activities were enhanced or inhibited by classroom configuration

- Incorporating learning resources such as active-learning facilitation kits into your small-group activities to enhance deep-learning experiences.

## KEY CONCEPTS

- Intentional space design can reinforce teaching strategies for deep learning.

- Thoughtful furniture and resource configurations help reveal learning goals to students.

- Students can make deep learning visible through collaborative space design.

- Learning galleries can make teaching for deep learning exciting.

## DISCUSSION QUESTIONS

1. In what ways can you transform a traditional classroom space into one that can enhance your teaching for deep learning?

2. In what ways might the positioning of chairs reveal deep learning strategies to students?

3. How might visual spaces contribute to deep learning?

4. What might the ideal space constructed for deep learning look like?

5. If you constructed the anti-deep learning space, what would it look like?

**BRIDLE: Creating Space**

Directions: Evaluate yourself.

Scale: 1=Very Strong, 2=Strong, 3=Moderate, 4=Weak, 5=Very Weak

| SCORE | DESCRIPTOR | COMMENTS |
|---|---|---|
|  | Understands importance of learning spaces and deep learning |  |
|  | Adapts classroom configuration to fit teaching goals |  |
|  | Incorporates learning experiences into small-group activities to enhance deep learning |  |
|  | Asks students for feedback on ways teaching activities were enhanced or inhibited by classroom configuration |  |
|  | Makes intervention intentional and reflective in the classroom configuration |  |

# REFERENCES

Boys, J. (2011). *Towards creative learning spaces: Re-Thinking the architecture of post-compulsory education.* New York: Routledge.

Carpenter, R. (2014). Negotiating the spaces of design in multimodal composition. *Computers and Composition: An International Journal, 33*(1): 68-78.

Carpenter, R. (Ed.). (2012). *Cases on higher education spaces: Innovation, collaboration, and technology.* Hershey, PA: IGI Global.

Carpenter, R. & Apostel, S. (2012). Communication center ethos: Remediating space, encouraging collaboration." in E. Yook & W. Atkins-Sayre (Eds.) *Communication Centers and Oral Communication Programs in Higher Education: Advantages, Challenges, and New Directions.* (161-174). Lanham, MD: Lexington Books.

Carpenter, R,, Selfe, D., Apostel, S. & Apostel, K. (Eds.). (2015). *Sustainable learning spaces: Design, infrastructure, and technology.* Logan, UT: Computers and

Composition Digital Press/Utah State University Press. Available from http://ccdigitalpress.org/ebooks-and-projects/sustainable>.

Carpenter, R., Valley, L., Napier, T. & and Apostel S. (2013). Studio pedagogy: A model for collaboration, innovation, and space design." In R. Carpenter (Ed.), *Cases on Higher Education Spaces: Innovation, Collaboration, and Technology.* (313-329). Hershey, PA: IGI Global.

Fairchild, J. & Carpenter, R. (2015). Embracing collaborative opportunities: Examining an ePortfolio bootcamp." *Communication Center Journal.* 1.1: 61-71.

Gardner, B., Napier, T., & Carpenter, R. (2013). "Reinventing library spaces and services: Harnessing campus partnerships to initiate and sustain transformational change." In A. Woodsworth and W. Penniman (Eds.). *Mergers and Alliances: The Operational View and Cases (Advances in Librarianship, Volume 37) (131-151).* n.p. Emerald Group Publishing Limited.

Lee, S., Alfano, C. & Carpenter, R. (2012). Invention in two parts: multimodality and space design in the writing center. In R. Carpenter (Ed.) *Cases on Higher Education Spaces: Innovation, Collaboration, and Technology* (41-63). Hershey, PA: IGI Global.

McWilliam, E., Sweet, C., & Blythe, H. (2013). "Re/membering pedagogical spaces." in R. Carpenter (Ed.) *Cases on Higher Education Spaces: Innovation, Collaboration, and Technology (1-43)*. Hershey, PA: IGI Global.

Oblinger, D. (Ed.). (2006). *Learning Spaces*. EDUCAUSE. Available from http://net.educause.edu/ir/library/pdf/PUB7102.pdf.

Sweet, C., Carpenter, R., Blythe, H. & Apostel, S. (2013). *Teaching applied creative thinking: A new pedagogy for the 21$^{st}$ century*. Stillwater, OK: New Forums Press.

# 12. STRATEGY VIII: Motivating Students To Be Deep Learners

**LEARNING QUIZ** (True or False)

1. Deep learners are intrinsically motivated.

2. Deep learners are extrinsically motivated.

3. As students move from elementary to higher education, they become more intrinsically motivated.

4. Providing students with a rationale to succeed works.

5. The only way to motivate students is to provide emotional speeches to them.

## BACKGROUND

*We've become increasingly aware that if students aren't motivated to learn, even the best practices will fail—or, at least, produce minimal returns.*

Over our years of mentoring colleagues, we've run into a situation that impacts this book. Often the mentored teacher will claim to have read our books, implemented our tips, but still found the students' performance lacking. "Why?" s/he asks. We've become increasingly aware that if students aren't motivated to learn, even the best practices will fail—or, at least, produce minimal returns.

Unfortunately, when we introduce the need for motivating students, we often receive this reaction: "Look, with all that I have to teach in class, I don't have time to motivate them to learn."

How many times have we all heard an instructor argue along these same lines? Consider someone in an allied field, a coach, at any level from T-Ball to the pros, trying to make the same argument. Effective coaches teach the basic skills and rules, but before putting players on the field or court, they must encourage them with more than a "Win one for the Gipper" speech—players must be given a reason to succeed. Back in *Achieving Excellence in Teaching* (2014), we stated simply that like the coach "the mentor serves as a motivator, inspiring students to reach their highest potential" (61).

Several elements are required for successful educational motivation:

Students must <u>want</u> to learn.

1. Students must <u>believe</u> they can learn. Students not receptive to the possibility that learning can be transformative are more apt to choose surface over deep learning.

2. Students must <u>believe that their teachers</u> can help them. As McGuire (2015) says, "When students become aware that their instructors have provided criticism in order to help them improve rather than as a judgment of their ostensibly fixed abilities, they are likelier to use that criticism constructively" (64). A student's positive mindset vs. **bellignorance** (see Chapter 3) plays a key role in their being able to be motivated.

3. Teachers must use <u>proven tactics</u> to motivate the students—i.e., academic stewardship.

4. Teachers must have the <u>proper dispositions/attitudes</u> to foster deep learning—passion and rapport (see our *Achieving Excellence in Teaching* for a fuller explanation). Lubin (2003), for instance, stresses, "a most potent way to encourage enthusiasm and interest in subjects is to demonstrate your own enthusiasm and interest in the subject" (25), and Walsh and Maffei (1996) believe that instructor-student rapport increases motivation and performance.

5. Teachers must provide an <u>explanation</u> of their rationale.

This book is designed to help you transform your students into deep learners, and to accomplish this task you may have to in part change your students from being extrinsically (e.g., Charlie was told by his parents who were paying for his education he couldn't purchase a new car unless his first-year GPA was 2.4 or better) to intrinsically motivated (e.g., eventually, he earned a Ph.D. without any external motivation). Research has shown that intrinsically motivated students learn more deeply. Research has also demonstrated another gap: for unknown reasons elementary students begin with intrinsic motivation, but it drops from grades 3-9 (Harter, 1981), so by the time they reach college, you can guess where the needle on the motivation-meter rests.

*Research has shown that intrinsically motivated students learn more deeply.*

## TACTICS FOR MOTIVATING STUDENTS TO BE DEEP LEARNERS

Can concerned faculty members actually help bring about a motivational change in their students from extrinsic to intrinsic? Fink (2013) calls this skill **leadership** — "motivating and enabling others to do important things well" (286) — and he emphasizes that "simply telling students on the first day of the course, 'I believe this subject is important; now here is a lecture on topic one,' clearly will not suffice to excite them to high-quality learning" (286). Grayling (2015) concludes, "a good teacher can ... give students the desire to know more, understand more, achieve greater insight. In short: the good teacher inspires" through "enthusiasm, charisma, a capacity to clarify and make sense, humor, kindness, and a genuine interest in students' progress" (B4). In order to achieve deep learning in students, the instructor must be certain that motivation is supported by the approach at presenting the material (see Chapter 6).

McGuire supplies four strategies to help students prepare to change their mindset so as to become better students:

1. "Inspire belief."

2. "Ask your students to recall other challenges they have overcome."

3. "Explain the neurobiological basis of the growth mindset—namely, brain plasticity."

4. "Help students achieve gradual, persistent growth" (68).

Ambrose et al (2010) believe student motivation is influenced by three major elements:

1. "**Value**. How important do I find this goal?"

2. "**Nature of the environment**. Do I feel supported or unsupported?"

3. "**Belief in the ability to succeed**. Do I believe I can design and follow a course of action to meet this goal?"

Lepper and Hodell (1989) provide four approaches for enhancing intrinsic motivation:

- **Challenge**: Provide assignments and exercises just above students' skill levels, but not so far above as to be impossible.

- **Curiosity**: Select assignments and exercises that provide slight discrepancies from what students already know/value.

- **Control**: Offer assignments and exercises wherein students can make a series of choices.

- **Fantasy**: Find sims (simulations) and games that are embedded with desired knowledge.

Borrowing from Lepper and Hodell, Turner and Paris (1995) created the Six Cs of Motivation:

- **Choice**: Allow students to select assignments and exercises based on their personal values and emotions.

- **Challenge**: see above

- **Control**: see above

- **Collaboration**: In our *Introduction to Applied Creative Thinking* (2012), Chapter X is devoted to collaborating. The key is concurrence on a goal by the collaborators as well as practice in working together.

- **Constructing Meaning**: Recommended for upper-division courses, this tactic depends on students recognizing the value of knowledge.

- **Consequences**: Figure out some simple rewards to recognize their work, such as publishing their self-created sonnets on the classroom wall or electronic repositories.

To these Cs, we would add one more: **Competition**. If you play games such as Jeopardy or Survivor, someone has to win, whether determined by teacher, class, or outsider vote. Competition does not have to be cutthroat, nor are teams forbidden.

Aligning themselves with some of the basic principles already enumerated, McKay and Kember (1997) claim, "faculty interested in deep learning should ask these questions," and among their six they list two important points about motivation:

- "Is the homework assignment sufficiently motivating with an emphasis on intrinsic motivation and a sense of 'ownership' of the material, often brought on by choice?"

- "Have I designed a motivating reward system that builds in individual accountability, but encourages cooperation?" (4).

Eventually a deep approach seems to engender motivating emotions in itself. Howie and Bagnall (2013) state, "A deep approach to learning typically has students feeling a positive regard for the subject matter with which they are engaged and, as they engage with it, having feelings of challenge, exhilaration, interest, pleasure and importance in relation to it" (390).

## A DON'T-FORGET-TO-DO ITEM

Day One, as we have said elsewhere, serves as the most important moment of the semester. Save some time so that after getting to know your students and going through the syllabus (emphasizing your daily quiz policy and the reasons for it) with them you can establish a few points:

1. We are all in this class together.

2. I am very heavily invested in your success.

3. I know you can succeed if you want to succeed and you follow the simple **ARTS** system (see Appendix C):

   - **A**ttend every class.

   - **R**ead every assignment carefully (and if they have reading problems, let them know where on campus they can get help).

   - **T**ake notes by hand.

   - **S**tudy later in the day for the class, making an effort to reorganize and prioritize items in your notes.

4. Here is my goal in this class.

5. Here is a short and simplified introduction to metacognition strategies (spend 15 minutes on this subject, and they will ask you for more time on the subject throughout the semester).

If you are find motivation difficult, start by trying to **empathize** with your students. Try to recall when you were in a similar class back in the day. If that tactic doesn't work, plumb your memory for that one special teacher who motivated you to become more than you thought you could be.

Today that teacher is you.

## KEY CONCEPTS

- **Motivation** is an important part of your responsibility as an instructor and leader.

- Transforming students from being extrinsically motivated to being intrinsically motivated fosters deep learning.

- The first class session is essential in motivating students to engage in deep learning.

- The teacher's instructional dispositions and actions strongly impact student motivation throughout the semester.

## DISCUSSION QUESTIONS

1. Perform a self-analysis of what motivates you to accomplish tasks, especially teaching. Would you consider yourself typical? Do you see any triggers in yourself that may be present in your students?

2. Being motivational is not a one-time item. Can you picture a basketball coach teaching a player a proper defensive stance and never

bringing it up again? Motivation is needed the most when students are most vulnerable. Other than on day one, what times in the semester would you expect to find students at peak vulnerability?

**BRIDLE: Motivating Students to Become Deep Learners**

Directions: Evaluate yourself.

Scale: 1=Very Strong, 2=Strong, 3=Moderate, 4=Weak, 5=Very Weak

| SCORE | DESCRIPTOR | COMMENTS |
|---|---|---|
| | Uses first class session to motivate students to engage in deep learning | |
| | Models motivation dispositions throughout the semester | |
| | Demonstrates through actions a commitment to motivating students | |
| | Encourages students away from extrinsic motivation toward intrinsic with such strategies as ARTS | |
| | Designs motivating reward system that builds in individual responsibility | |

# REFERENCES

Ambrose, S., Bridges, M., DiPietro, M., Lovett, M. & Norman, M. (2010). *How learning works: Seven research-based principles for smart teaching.* San Francisco: Jossey-Bass.

Fink, L. (2013). *Creating significant learning experiences.* San Francisco: Jossey-Bass.

Grayling, A. (2015, December). What makes a good teacher. *The Chronicle Review*, 11, B4.

Harter, S. (1981). A new self-report scale of intrinsic versus extrinsic orientation in the Classroom: Motivational and informational components. *Developmental Psychology*, *17*(3), 300-312.

Howie, P., & Bagnall, R. (2013). A critique of deep and surface approaches to learning model. *Teaching in Higher Education, 18*(4), 389-400.

Lepper, M., & Hodell, M. (1989). Intrinsic motivation in the classroom. In C. Ames & R. Ames (Eds.), *Research on Motivation in Education* (Vol. 3, pp. 73-105). San Diego: Academic Press.

Lubin, J. (2003, October). *Deep, surface and strategic approaches to learning.* Online Document from UCD Dublin Centre for Teaching and Learning. Retrieved from http://www2.warwick.ac.uk/services/ide/development/pga/introandl/resources/2a_deep_surfacestrategic_approaches_to_learning.pdf

McGuire, S. & McGuire, S. J. (2015). *Teach students how to learn.* Sterling, VA: Stylus.

McKay, J., & Kember, D. (1997). Spoon feeding leads to regurgitation: A better diet can result in more digestible learning outcomes. *Higher Education Research and Development, 6*(1), 55-67.

Sweet, C., Blythe, H., & Carpenter, R. (2012). *Introduction to applied creative thinking.* Stillwater, OK: New Forums Press.

Sweet, C., Blythe, H., Phillips, B., Daniel, C. (2014). *Achieving excellence in teaching.* Stillwater, OK: New Forums Press.

Walsh, D., & Maffei, M. (1996). Never in a class by themselves: An examination of the Behaviors affecting student-professor relationship. *Essays on Teaching Excellence—Professional and Organizational Development Network, 7*(2), 1.

# Part III

## Honing Your Skills

# 13. Conclusion

*"Yes, I understand you would be more comfortable nearer the surface when we have class."*

As the cartoon suggests, students entering higher education have been reared on and rewarded for surface learning. To succeed at the college level, they must acquire the deep learning skills explored in this book. Sandover, Jonas-Dwyer, and Marr (2015) report, "Research has shown that students who adopt a deep learning approach perform better in coursework and project work, are more satisfied with their course and do better in exams." Furthermore, research has demonstrated that due to neuroplasticity— i.e., the brain's ability to grow and change — students possess the ability to rewire their K-12- and societal-trained brains, though Marton and Saljo (1997) discovered transforming students into deep learners not an easy task.

This book has been designed to provide dedicated instructors with a methodology for effecting a change in their students' depth of learning. Moreover, through BRIDLE these instructors can monitor their own progress in achieving this goal. Our attempt, as we have noted, is to provide a simplified and synthesized approach rather than a comprehensive treatment of the subject. We have found that busy, overworked instructors desirous of such a change want a practical process that will inform their preparation and presentation, even assessment.

If you'd like to build a strong bridge across the learning gap, this book is for you.

# REFERENCES

Marton, F. & Saljo, R. Approaches to learning. In N. Entwhistle (Ed.) *Approaches to Learning*. Edinburgh: Scottish Academic Press.

Sandover, S., Jonas-Dwyer, D., & Marr, T. (2015). Graduate entry and undergraduate medical students' study approaches, stress levels and ways of coping: a Five-year longitudinal study. *BMC Medical Education, 15*(5). DOI 10.1186/s12909-015-0284-7.

# 14. APPENDIX A: BRIDLE, A Systematic Plan for Self-Improvement in Promoting Deep Learning

BRIDLE, or the Basic Rubric for Improving Deep Learning Education, is meant to function as a self-help instrument for faculty interested in evaluating their skills and strategies for deep learning. While each appeared separately in the respective chapters of our EIGHT EXCELLENT STRATEGIES FOR DEEP LEARNING, here we present a compilation for easy use. In fact, after reading the book and implementing the strategies, you might want to use this collection as a post-test. Furthermore, if you are interested in triangulation, you could give a colleague who has observed you, consulted with you, or simply read through your teaching portfolio a chance to evaluate you, and you could even use the entire mechanism or part of it for student evaluation of your teaching.

**BRIDLE: Bloom**

Directions: Evaluate yourself.

Scale: 1=Very Strong, 2=Strong, 3=Moderate, 4=Weak, 5=Very Weak

| SCORE | DESCRIPTOR | COMMENTS |
|---|---|---|
| | SLOs reflect an emphasis on higher-order over lower-order skills | |
| | Assignments (in and out of class) reflect an emphasis on higher-order over lower-order skills | |
| | Assessments (tests, papers) reflect an emphasis on higher-order over lower-order skills | |
| | Class discussions promote the use of higher-order skills | |
| | Rationale is intentionally provided to the students on the importance of Bloom's Taxonomy in deep learning | |

## BRIDLE: Presenting

Directions: Evaluate yourself.

Scale: 1=Very Strong, 2=Strong, 3=Moderate, 4=Weak, 5=Very Weak

| SCORE | DESCRIPTOR | COMMENTS |
|---|---|---|
|  | Effectively uses the mini-lecture rather than the full-period lecture |  |
|  | Provides time for students' active learning through group/solitary in-class work |  |
|  | Provides time for students' active learning through oral/written reflection |  |
|  | Views self as co-facilitator with the student of deep learning |  |
|  | Utilizes the C.R.I.S.P. approach to deep learning |  |

## BRIDLE: Retrieving

Directions: Evaluate yourself.

Scale: 1=Very Strong, 2=Strong, 3=Moderate, 4=Weak, 5=Very Weak

| SCORE | DESCRIPTOR | COMMENTS |
|---|---|---|
|  | Intentionally instructs students as to the best practices in retrieving strategies |  |
|  | Provides frequent retrieval opportunities inside and outside of class |  |
|  | Offers immediate feedback (when feasible) after student retrieving efforts |  |
|  | Offers opportunities for practice testing and reflection |  |
|  | Offers frequent opportunities for S3P strategies |  |

## BRIDLE: Metacognition

Directions: Evaluate yourself.

Scale: 1=Very Strong, 2=Strong, 3=Moderate, 4=Weak, 5=Very Weak

| SCORE | DESCRIPTOR | COMMENTS |
|---|---|---|
| | Intentionally teaches metacognitive strategies to students | |
| | Intentionally teaches the mindset concept to students early in course | |
| | Uses the ARTS (or a version of it) to help students monitor their development | |
| | Uses metacognitive strategies to foster students' abilities to teach themselves | |
| | | |

## BRIDLE: Critical Thinking

Directions: Evaluate yourself.

Scale: 1=Very Strong, 2=Strong, 3=Moderate, 4=Weak, 5=Very Weak

| SCORE | DESCRIPTOR | COMMENTS |
|---|---|---|
| | Utilizes effective critical thinking practices such as the 20+-page paper, debates, and 40 pages of reading/week | |
| | Teaches evaluating the argument through **PASSOR**—Perspective | |
| | Teaches evaluating the argument through **PASSOR**--Accuracy | |
| | Teaches evaluating the argument through **PASSOR**--Sufficiency | |
| | Teaches evaluating the argument through **PASSOR**--Specificity | |
| | Teaches evaluating the argument through **PASSOR**--Objectivity | |
| | Teaches evaluating the argument through **PASSOR**--Relevance | |

## BRIDLE: Deep Reading for Deep Learning

Directions: Evaluate yourself.

Scale: 1=Very Strong, 2=Strong, 3=Moderate, 4=Weak, 5=Very Weak

| SCORE | DESCRIPTOR | COMMENTS |
|---|---|---|
| | Provides students practice in applying PASSOR to their reading | |
| | Teaches several tactics of deep reading | |
| | Helps students recognize the required reading speed for various assignments | |
| | Acquaints students with a given discipline's fundamental and powerful concepts | |
| | Makes use of paper texts | |

## BRIDLE: Creating Spaces for Deep Learning

Directions: Evaluate yourself.

Scale: 1=Very Strong, 2=Strong, 3=Moderate, 4=Weak, 5=Very Weak

| SCORE | DESCRIPTOR | COMMENTS |
|---|---|---|
| | Understands importance of learning spaces and deep learning | |
| | Adapts classroom configuration to fit teaching goals | |
| | Incorporates learning experiences into small-group activities to enhance deep learning | |
| | Asks students for feedback on ways teaching activities were enhanced or inhibited by classroom configuration | |
| | Makes intervention intentional and reflective in the classroom configuration | |

## BRIDLE: Motivating Students to Become Deep Learners

Directions: Evaluate yourself.

Scale: 1=Very Strong, 2=Strong, 3=Moderate, 4=Weak, 5=Very Weak

| SCORE | DESCRIPTOR | COMMENTS |
|---|---|---|
|  | Uses first class session to motivate students to engage in deep learning |  |
|  | Models motivation dispositions throughout the semester |  |
|  | Demonstrates through actions a commitment to motivating students |  |
|  | Encourages students away from extrinsic motivation toward intrinsic with such strategies as ARTS |  |
|  | Designs motivating reward system that builds in individual responsibility |  |

# 15. APPENDIX B: An Annotated Bibliography for Further Reading and Research

**By Brittany Biddle-Brandenburg, Eastern Kentucky University**

Part of my job as the Graduate Research Assistant for the Teaching & Learning Center and the Noel Studio for Academic Creativity is to provide the authors with up-to-date research that can assist instructors with the knowledge and tools they need to transform their students into deep learners. This work is subtitled *A Guide for Instructors*, so it was interesting to be in the student role as I gathered relevant research for this book. While researching deep learning, I found several key takeaways, including:

1. Most college students are highly underprepared by their teachers in high school to perform well. Not only are their reading levels frighteningly low, but they know only how to read for factual information that can be spat back when prompted, and they do not know how to *learn*.

2. Colleges may actually be promoting surface, or shallow, learning. Because institutions are emphasizing the importance of grades, GPAs, and graduation within four years, students are no longer concerned with *learning*, but with putting in the minimal effort necessary to achieve a respectable GPA and a degree in four years.

3. A student's mindset is a key variable in whether s/he can be transformed into a deep learner or not. Students with a fixed mindset could potentially be too discouraged by the possibility of failure if they change their reading strategy. Thus, teachers are a crucial mechanism in transitioning students from a **fixed mindset** to a **growth mindset**.

4. No surefire strategies that instructors can teach their students in order to turn them into deep learners exist, and not every strategy will work for every student. Rather, experimentation and a trial-and-error approach with the various methods discussed in this book is recommended.

5. If deep learning and deep reading are the expectation, then these goals need to be what is rewarded, and teachers can do their part by explaining each reading's relevance to the topic. Such gestures will entice the students to read more deeply and embed the ideas into their semantic memory, a key component of deep learning.

The following pages contain some of the resources I gathered pertaining to deep learning. Finding some of the resources especially rewarding, I provided annotations for them. I hope you find them as worthwhile as I did. Good luck transforming your students into deep learners!

ACT. (2006). Executive Summary. In *Reading between the lines: What the ACT reveals about college readiness in reading.* Retrieved from http://www.act.org/research/policymakers/pdf/reading_summary.pdf

Associated Press. (2006, January 20). *Reports on college literacy level sobering.* Retrieved from http://www.nbcnews.com/id/10928755/ns/us_news-education/t/reports-college-literacy-levels-sobering/#.VjoNDLerTcs

Baer, J. D., Cook, A. L. Baldi, S. (2006). Executive Summary. In *The literacy of America's college students.* Retrieved from http://www.air.org/sites/default/files/downloads/report/The20Literacy20of20Americas20College20Students_final20report_0.pdf

Brown, P., Roediger, H. & McDaniel, M. (2014). *Make it stick: The science of successful learning.* Cambridge, MA: The Belknap Press of Harvard University Press.

- Brown, Roediger, and McDaniel wrote *Make It Stick* to show people, namely students and teachers, what they can do for themselves in order to learn better and have better memories. Using cognitive psychology and other related disciplines, the authors propose several techniques that people can use to become more "productive learners." The authors write that for many students the act of studying involves cramming sessions, underlining and highlighting sections of text, rereading passages in the hopes that the repetition alone will make it stick. These actions lead to what the authors call the "illusion of mastery." Students may feel that they have truly learned the material after studying this way — and, in fact they may actually perform well on exams — but the material is not actually learned for the long term. In order for students to really learn material and ensure its retention for the long term, the authors argue for more complex and durable learning to take place through self-testing, creating purposely challenging practice scenarios, restudying new material only after forgetting has started to take place, and interleaving, or incorporating, one skill or topic with others. Using a story-telling approach, the authors provide ample examples of strategies for mastery learning. Readers will find that the organization of the book also parallels two main ideas of the book — the repetition of key ideas and the interleaving of related topics — as it illustrates the strategies for true mastery learning.

Cal Poly. (n.d.). *Supporting student success*. Retrieved from http://www.cosam.calpoly.edu/content/student_success

Carr, N. (2010). *The shallows*. New York, NY: W. W. Norton & Company, Inc.

- In *The Shallows*, Carr writes that while the Internet is a great tool and resource, it could be our very demise, interfering with our ability to read and think deeply. According to Carr, the Internet is encouraging us to only sample small bits of information, causing us to be skilled at skimming information but decreasing our ability to concentrate and reflect, key components of deep learning. This deleterious effect is not exclusive to the Internet, however. In *The Shallows*, Carr discusses several other new technological tools and their effects on society. The Internet is promoting shallow learning when deep learning is more desirable. Carr uses neurological science to explain the biological effect of the Internet on our brains and our capacity to learn.

Cook, E., Kennedy, E., & McGuire, S. (2013). Effect of teaching metacognitive learning strategies on performance in general chemistry courses. *Journal of Chemical Education, 90*, 961-967.

DeLoatch, P. (2015, May 2). The four negative sides of technology. Retrieved from http://www.edudemic.com/the-4-negative-sides-effects-of-technology/

Dweck, C. (2006). *Mindset: The new psychology of success*. New York: Ballentine.

- In *Mindset: The New Psychology of Success*, Dweck investigates why some people are discouraged by a challenge while others thrive. Dweck explains that it is people's mindset — how they think about intelligence and how it is acquired — that affects the way they live their life. A fixed mindset believes that human qualities are concrete and unchanging. Intelligence, personality, and moral character are set in stone, and absolutely no room to reshape those human qualities with this mindset exists. On the contrary, the growth mindset believes that individual effort can change those same human qualities. For students receiving a poor grade, these mindsets are the difference between students saying, "I'm a total failure" (fixed mindset) and "I need to try harder/study differently next time" (growth mindset). Mindsets are important because they affect how individuals — students in particular — view success, interest, and failure. Those with a fixed mindset opt for success over growth, preferring to take the easy road to ensure they succeed. They become disinterested in a topic when it becomes too challenging because the possibility of failure is now greater. Those with a growth mindset, on the other hand, view learning and development as success, preferring to challenge themselves and becoming more interested in a topic when it is challenging. Dweck ends the book by explaining that mindsets can be changed and instructs teachers how to be great. The key to changing a fixed mindset to a growth mindset is to transition from a "judge-and-be-judged" framework to a "learn-and-help-learn" framework. Teachers who regularly communicate the latter framework can help students change their fixed mindset into a growth mindset by setting high standards and helping their students reach them.

Edelstein, D. (2000, July 12). *Tests + stress = problems for students*. Retrieved from http://brainconnection.branhq.com/2000/07/12/tests-stress-problems-for-students/

Frodl, T. & O'Keane, V. (2013). How does the brain deal with cumulative stress? A review with focus on development stress, HPA axis function and hippocampal structure in humans. *Neurobiology of Disease, 52,* 24-37. DOI: 10.1016.j.nbd.2012.03.012

Hope, M. (2015, January 3). *Expert: Most US college freshmen read at 7th grade level*. Retrieved from http://www.breitbart.com/texas/2015/01/03/expert-most-us-college-freshmen-read-at-7th-grade-level/

Johnson, J. (2013, September 14). *Today's typical college students often juggle work, children, and bills with coursework.* Retrieved from https://www.washingtonpost.com/local/education/todays-typical-college-students-often-juggle-children-and-bills-with-coursework/2013/09/14/4158c8c0-1718-11e3-804b-d3a1a3a18f2c_story.html

Karpicke, J. (2012). Retrieval-based learning: Active retrieval promotes meaningful learning. *Current Directions in Psychological Science, 21*(3), 157-163.

Ken Jennings. (n.d.). Retrieved from http://en.m.wikipedia.org/wiki/Ken_Jennings

Kornell, N., Hays, M., & Bjork, R. (2009). Unsuccessful retrieval attempts enhance subsequent learning. *Journal of Experimental Psychology: learning, memory, and cognition, 35*(4), 989-998.

McGuire, S. & McGuire, S. (2015). *Teach students how to learn.* Sterling, VA: Stylus.

- I had the privilege of hearing one of Dr. McGuire's lectures on metacognition in the fall of 2015. A metacognition guru, she travels the country, instructing students to become better learners and offering teachers resources and strategies to teach their students how to learn.

What stood out to me most when I attended Dr. McGuire's lecture is the substantial difference between *studying* and *learning*. McGuire's book *Teach Students How to Learn* is for teachers who find themselves responsible for teaching underprepared students who lack the ability to learn, are unmotivated, and disengaged. McGuire focuses on the three M's — mindset, motivation, and metacognition — and in *Teach Students How to Learn,* McGuire offers specific and useful strategies backed by science to teach students how to learn and not simply study. McGuire ends the book by reminding her audience that no right or wrong approaches to teaching students how to learn exist and that not every strategy works for every student. Instead, she encourages teachers and students alike to experiment with various strategies in order to see what works best for them.

Orlin, B. (2013, September 9). *When memorization gets in the way of learning.* Retrieved from http://www.theatlantic.com/education/archive/2013/09/when-memorization-gets-in-the-way-of-learning/279425/

Roberts, J. & Roberts, K. (2008). Deep reading, cost/benefit, and the construction of meaning: Enhancing reading comprehension and deep learning in sociology courses. *Teaching Sociology, 36,* 25-140.

- Roberts and Roberts offer a definition for deep reading as reading for long-term retention and comprehension of the material in a way that transforms perspectives. The authors suggest that college students need help developing deep reading strategies. In high school these students were reading for factual information that could easily be regurgitated later, but in college reading to make meaning or construct an argument or thesis (deep learning) is more desirable. Because college students lack this skill, they often forego the reading assignments. Roberts and Roberts write that it may be the student culture that is promoting shallow, or surface, reading and learning techniques. Colleges stress credits and degrees as well as the value of a good GPA as opposed to the value of topic mastery. If the higher-order skills of Bloom's Taxonomy are not required, then deep reading will not occur. The authors summarize the literature to explain that reading for meaning requires engagement with the material so that it can be encoded into semantic memory. Simply explaining to students the benefits of deep reading and costs of surface reading will not lead to deep reading if the outcome goals (which promote surface learning) do not change. The authors offer a strategy to be followed when reading assignments are given, and evidence of success is presented.

Rooconi, L., Ribera, A., & Laird, T. (2014, November). College seniors' plans for graduate school: Do deep approaches to learning and Holland academic environments matter? *Research in Higher Education.* DOI: 10.1007/s11162-014-9358-3.

Scouller, K. (1998). The influence of assessment method on students' learning approaches: Multiple choice question examination versus assignment essay. *Higher Education, 35,* 453-472.

Stanger-Hall, K. F. (2012). Multiple-choice exams: An obstacle for higher-level thinking in introductory science classes. *Cell Biology Education— Life Sciences Education,* 11 (3), 294-306.

Tanner, K. D. (2012). Promoting student metacognition. *CBE — Life Sciences Education, 11,* 113-120.

Towler, L. (2014, November 25). *Deeper learning: Moving students beyond memorization.* Retrieved from http://neattoday.org/2014/11/25/deeper-learning-moving-students-beyond-moemorization-2/

Weimer, M. (2012). *Deep learning vs. surface learning: Getting students to understand the difference.* Retrieved from http://www.facultyfocus.com/articles/teaching-professor-blog/deep-learning-vs-surface-learning-getting-students-to-understand-the-difference/

Zhao, N., Wardeska, J. G., McGuire, S. Y., & Cook, E. (2014). Metacognition: An effective tool to promote success in college science learning. *Journal of College Science Learning, 43*(4),48-54.

# Appendix C: ARTS

|  | OFTEN | SOMETIMES | SELDOM | NEVER |
|---|---|---|---|---|
| **ATTENDANCE** | | | | |
| 1. I attend every class of every course I take. | | | | |
| 2. I arrive early. | | | | |
| 3. I sit in the front row. | | | | |
| 4. I participate in class discussions | | | | |
| 5. I bring my book to class. | | | | |
| 6. I bring a notebook to class. | | | | |

|  | OFTEN | SOMETIMES | SELDOM | NEVER |
|---|---|---|---|---|
| **READING** | | | | |
| 1. I preview my assigned reading. | | | | |
| 2. I know when to read the material slowly/fast. | | | | |
| 3. I underline key passages. | | | | |
| 4. I scribble notes on the readings' pages. | | | | |
| 5. I relate what is new in texts to what I know. | | | | |
| 6. I believe rereading is the best way to learn. | | | | |

|  | OFTEN | SOMETIMES | SELDOM | NEVER |
|---|---|---|---|---|
| **TAKING NOTES** | | | | |
| 1. I take notes in class by hand. | | | | |
| 2. As I write, I organize my notes. | | | | |
| 3. I note things that I don't fully understand. | | | | |
| 4. I make comments in my notes. | | | | |
| 5. I tie today's notes with previous material. | | | | |
| 6. After class I rewrite my notes. | | | | |

|  | OFTEN | SOMETIMES | SELDOM | NEVER |
|---|---|---|---|---|
| **STUDYING** | | | | |
| 1. I study every day, averaging over 10 hours/week. | | | | |
| 2. I make up flashcards for key concepts. | | | | |
| 3. I study with a group. | | | | |
| 4. I cram all my studying in right before the test. | | | | |
| 5. I create practice tests on the material. | | | | |
| 6. I eliminate distractions (cells, TV, computer). | | | | |

# ABOUT THE AUTHORS

**Charlie Sweet**, Ph.D. (Florida State University, 1970), is the Co-Director of the Teaching & Learning Center at Eastern Kentucky University. With Hal, he has collaborated on over 1100 published works, including 19 books, literary criticism, educational research, and novels (as Quinn MacHollister).

**Hal Blythe**, Ph.D. (University of Louisville, 1972), is the Co-Director of the Teaching & Learning Center. With Charlie, he has collaborated on over 1100 published works, including 19 books (eight in New Forums' popular It Works For Me series), literary criticism, educational research, and a stint as ghostwriter of the lead novella for the *Mike Shayne Mystery Magazine*.

**Bill Phillips**, Ed.D., (University of Southern Mississippi, 1988), is former Dean of the College of Education at Eastern Kentucky University and a collaborator on *Achieving Excellence in Teaching*, 2014.

**Russell Carpenter**, Ph.D. (University of Central Florida, 2009), is Executive Director of the Noel Studio for Academic Creativity and Program Director of Applied Creative Thinking at Eastern Kentucky University where he is also Associate Professor of English. Dr. Carpenter has published on the topic of creative thinking, among other areas, including three texts by New Forums Press: *Introduction to Applied Creative Thinking* (with Charlie Sweet and Hal Blythe, 2012), *Teaching Applied Creative Thinking* (with Charlie Sweet, Hal Blythe, and Shawn Apostel, 2013), and *It Works for Me, Flipping the Classroom: Shared Tips for Effective Teaching*, (with Hal Blythe and Charlie Sweet, 2015). He has guest edited or co-edited special issues of the *Journal of Faculty Development* on social media and the future of faculty development. In addition, he has taught courses in creative thinking in EKU's Minor in Applied Creative Thinking, which was featured in the *New York Times* in February 2014, and rhetoric and composition in the Department of English.

www.ingramcontent.com/pod-product-compliance
Lightning Source LLC
Chambersburg PA
CBHW062132160426
43191CB00013B/2277